PRAISE FOR THE BOOK

"This book is not only for learned saints and scholars but also for those looking for content which is easy to absorb. It is extremely well written and will benefit those seeking wisdom. People today are talking abut science and spirituality. This book brings out the direct connection between the two. A laudable book … a call to the younger generation dedicated to self-transformation."

O. P. Mehra, Air Chief Marshal (Retd.), Padma Vibhushan, Former Governor of Maharashtra & Rajasthan.

"This book enables you to discover who you are and what is the meaning and purpose of your life. The answers are found both from spiritual and scientific perspectives. But more than that, it is full of practical wisdom to guide your actions in every day life. Every one who believes in action will find the book very useful."

Suresh Kumar, Vice Chairman, Jaypee Ventures Pvt. Ltd. – Jaiprakash Group.

"In today's fast paced world we go through the motions of life at the speed of lightening and are always engulfed in a rat-race. Examples of burn outs, nervous break-down, and depression are common. At the eve of our life when we look back, apart from materialistic rewards, the balance sheet of our soul is rather empty."

"Dr. Vaish in his most amazing book has in a very beautiful setting lucidly explained the search of our soul. The ability of Dr. Vaish in explaining things in a very simple and readable manner and yet grappling with complicated issues surrounding quantum physics, and old Indian scriptures, is manifest in this very interesting book."

"This is a must read for every individual of the 21st century."

Umesh Kumar Khaitan,
Eminent Lawyer & International consultant.

"This book is a message to all those who are searching a bridge between science and spirituality. It gives a new vision which the society needs in today's time."

Pawan Ji,
Astro-physicist & Astro-veda consultant.

"Dr. Vaish has described very well how in order to be happy, one must control his own action/reaction, only Inner Me can give happiness, how cooperation brings greater happiness than competition, and living under fear does not allow one to do his best. The book has been presented in a way that will appeal to younger generation. Should read it again and again, and bring change in life – and use it as a reference book".

M. H. Dalmia, President,
OCL India. Ltd. – Dalmia Group of Industries

"The story is interesting and significantly adds to the readability of a serious text. I found it very readable and the thoughts were not overly difficult to understand and assimilate. No doubt, a book of this sort would require more than one reading to fully understand and absorb the ethos."

Tilak Dhar, Chairman,
DCM Sriram Industries Ltd. – DCM Group

"There is a spiritual message – and journey and lessons along the way, but there is a certain comfort, calm and simplicity in which it does so that you do not have any major resistance to the ideas it puts to you. The concepts are sprinkled through the narrative … … good for new readers"

Akshay Dhar, Young Student

"This book deals with profound insight of inner self of a human being. It helps one to understand life in its true meaning. A very interesting book to understand one self, and thus lead a very contented and peaceful life in this strife ridden world."

Dr. Kusum Ansal,
celebrated writer and academician

"Dr. Vaish's "Search" is compelling, profound, deep and penetrative – it leaves you spell bound and at the same time motivates you to achieve that "Shivo-ham, Shivo-ham, Shivo-ham. That pure cosmic consciousness – That is me" – the state of perfect bliss and eternal peace so that "I am one with the eternal." The blending of science and spirituality is unique. A work which could flow only out of one's heart and in this case Dr. Vaish's."

Lalit Bhasin, Eminent lawyer, former President,
Bar Council of India, and Chairman, Society of Indian Law Firms.

"This book deals with questions such as: "Who am I? Why

we have so much conflict in our lives? What is my role and relationship in this inexplicable phenomenon called Existence?" In "Searching for Me" Dr. Ramesh Vaish has offered his insights into the answers to these questions. He has also connected his readers to many related fields of activity and achievements in our daily life. The answers beautifully integrate our knowledge both in spirituality and science.

I am amazed at his zeal and understanding of issues which have baffled and exercised great minds. The vast data-base he offers from beginning to end will take some quality time to be absorbed.

The central character in this book, Aparna, is a seeker with intensity and dedication. Her story could be the story of my own life. I am grateful that he asked me to write my comments which entailed my dipping into the ocean of great wisdom that he has so generously offered in this book."

Dr. Sonal Mansingh, Padma Vibhushan, and celebrated exponent of Indian dance.

"I truly believe this book will be well received by our broken Western Culture. Everyone is searching for answers." "As we pull ourselves up and out of some difficult times, Linda keeps quoting your book and gives us all hope. So already your book has made a big impact. What a treasure."

Mary Lavan, Social worker, USA.

SEARCHING FOR ME

SEARCHING FOR ME

RAMESH VAISH

STERLING

STERLING PAPERBACKS
An imprint of
Sterling Publishers (P) Ltd.
Regd. Office: A1/256 Safdarjung Enclave,
New Delhi-110029. CIN: U22110DL1964PTC211907
Tel: 26387070, 26386209
E-mail: mail@sterlingpublishers.in
www.sterlingpublishers.in

SEARCHING FOR ME
© 2018, Ramesh Vaish
ISBN 978 93 86245 23 6
First Edition 2011
First Reprint 2018

All rights are reserved.
No part of this publication may be reproduced, stored in a retrieval system or transmitted, in any form or by any means, mechanical, photocopying, recording or otherwise, without prior written permission of the original publisher.

Printed and Published in India by

Sterling Publishers Pvt. Ltd.,
Plot No. 13, Ecotech-III, Greater Noida - 201306, U. P. India

PREFACE AND ACKNOWLEDGEMENTS

THIS IS A STORY OF APARNA – a well-educated young medical doctor working in a renowned hospital. She lives in New Delhi with her husband Raj and son Varun. She is quite successful in her profession, yet she feels something is missing. This story is about her journey to find her true self.

Her search for her own identity begins to unfold through her experiences with people from many walks of life. The answers to her many questions come in unexpected ways through her interaction with patients, spiritual saints, yoga teachers, social workers, economists, astro-physicists, and many others.

Aparna's exploration of answers to some basic questions in her life, and her search for happiness and harmony, unfold some very practical wisdom for living in this world. She insists on pragmatic and scientifically verifiable answers – and finds them.

Her search also leads her to a beautiful blending of science and spirituality when she discovers the 'light', which unites them both. She connects with nature, establishes a lovely communication with the holy river Ganges, and discovers the essential attributes of a harmonious life – a life that keeps glowing like a flame and flowing like a river.

Aparna's story is very much like the story of each one of us. We also go through challenges and conflicts in our lives, and we face similar questions about our own identity and the meaning and purpose of our existence. We keep searching for real-life practical ways to respond to those situations, and we keep wondering why all the happiness and harmony keep slipping away from us. In her search, Aparna gets the answers, which may help us to find ours.

Through my long working life, which has spanned more than five decades, my own answers have gradually emerged. This book seeks to capture those answers. Every single thought and every interaction leading to an answer is based upon a real-life experience. Each character in the story is based on a real person but some names have been changed. Although it is written as Aparna's story, 'Searching for Me' is also a story about our own lives.

For making it possible for me to tell this story, I owe my gratitude to many who have inspired me and have allowed me to utilize their great knowledge and insights. In particular, I am grateful to Air Chief Marshall OP Mehra (retired.), Swami Chidanand Saraswati, Shri Pawan Ji, Maa Abha Saraswati, Dr. Alka and Devi Sadhwi Bhagwati. My daughter Smita has been a great help in keeping my thought process and expression clear. The editorial assistance provided by Amita Sarwal and Linda Homewood has been most valuable.

The ideas discussed in the book have come from some of the greatest minds of our times in the fields of philosophy, quantum physics, social sciences and spirituality. Those ideas and their invaluable works have been listed and acknowledged in the last section of the book in Notes and References. I owe my grateful thanks to these authors, scientists and philosophers.

Each of these ideas has a unique significance, beauty and charm. If the story of Aparna is able to show you a practical way to implement and utilize those ideas in your day-to-day life, this book will have achieved its purpose.

New Delhi, India **Ramesh Vaish**
June 12, 2011

POSTSCRIPT

Much water has flown down the Ganges since this book was written in 2011. It is quite encouraging that several ideas presented in the book have not only been recognized but further developed by some of the most learned scholars, scientists and philosophers. One such significant idea in this book that is relevant in the life of each one of us, is our ongoing process of Becoming leading to a new state of Being, and how this transformation is influenced and shaped by our environment and our own thoughts and beliefs.

Bruce Lipton,[1] the leading scientist in the field of new cell-biology and known for his pioneering work in bridging science and spirituality, has shown the interface between biological organisms and their environment and the influence of thought, perception and subconscious awareness on human body. He has questioned the "myth of genetic determinism", and has shown that it is our own beliefs that create every aspect of our personal reality. His work takes forward the science of Epigenetics, which shows how environmental signals select, modify and regulate gene activity and how one could change the character of life by changing one's beliefs. This opens the way to self-empowerment – through the knowledge of Self, and thereby, to the power to shape one's own life. Armed with this knowledge and power he, in his own words, asks the question and also gives the answer:

1   Bruce H. Lipton. *The Biology of Belief*.2017. Twenty-first Reprint, Hay House India.

"If I could be anybody, who would I be?"

And his answer: "For now, the answer is a no-brainer– I want to be me!"

The obvious question arises: Who is this "Me"?

In this book, Aparna is also searching for "Me". Her search eventually takes her to the holy river Ganges . . . and she finds her answer. Sure enough, you too can find yours, too!

Welcome to the story of Aparna's *Searching for Me*.

New Delhi, India **Ramesh Vaish**
June 12, 2018

Contents

	Praise for the Book	*3*
	Preface and Acknowledgements	*11*
	Postscript	*13*
CHAPTER 1	Who am I?	17
CHAPTER 2	Why the Conflict?	71
CHAPTER 3	What to do?	123
CHAPTER 4	How to be?	155
CHAPTER 5	Where are you going?	187
	Notes and References	*213*
	About the Author	*216*

CHAPTER 1

Who am I?

"DOCTOR, CAN YOU PLEASE HELP US?" The man asked me.

"Yes. Tell me, what is the problem?" I asked in a helpful voice.

A well-dressed young man and an attractive young woman were sitting in front of me in my clinic. They appeared to be a happily married couple. How could I help them, I wanted to know.

"Doctor, we have been married for seven years." The husband explained: "We are both 30 plus and I wish to have a baby now. We are well off, and can take good care of a baby. But my wife doesn't want that."

His wife kept quiet, as her husband continued: "This sometimes causes tension in our home. You see, if we delay this too long, I may be nearing my retirement age before the children finish their education and get settled. I see no point in delaying this further."

I turned my attention to his wife. She looked at her husband, and then said to me: "I understand what Dev is saying. I am also a working woman, and I have a full-time job in a bank. But, I do not feel happy, nor settled, and definitely not ready to bring another life into the family."

"Could you tell me why do you feel this way?" I asked. "Maybe I can be of some help."

She obviously felt reassured with my attitude, and opened up: "Doctor, we have been together for seven years, and we both work. But things here look so bad. There is so much stress in our work and so much tension in our lives. No one gets a fair deal, the system does not work, and we have to fight for everything. Even within the family, I do not get along very well with my in-laws. I see conflict all around us and it is so difficult to cope with that."

After a pause, she continued: "I have been telling Dev that we should move away to some other place. If we try, we can find decent jobs in America. My brother lives in California. He is asking us to come there and he is prepared to help, but Dev does not want to go. All this is very frustrating for me. How can I have a baby? It would be very unfair to the baby if we are not able to solve our own problems in life before we bring a baby to join us. I do not even know what is the meaning of my own life and my work, and why are we living like this in so much of conflict?"

With an air of firmness, she then said: "We want so many things in life. But we should know when we are ready – when we can afford them. I don't think I can afford to have a baby at this time in my life."

I did not know what to say. It was obvious that she had closed the conversation. Behind the firmness of her voice, I could feel a deep sense of frustration. I looked at Dev. He looked disappointed and helpless, but said nothing.

Dev had also indicated to me that she had lost all interest in her marital life. I did a clinical examination and found nothing wrong. I just gave her a mild prescription for taking care of her stress and fatigue. I also gave her counseling on childbirth and its emotional significance for the parents. I tried to explain how a baby in the family can change the environment and bring so much happiness to the parents.

They never came back to me, but I could not forget the frustrated look of the young woman and her words of dismay at the situation around her. I also realized my own feeling of helplessness in dealing with her situation. That night, I thought of her as I got into bed, and it occurred to me that my own situation was not very different. I experience similar frustration when I see conflict all around me. Sometimes, my entire struggle for success seems futile, and I keep wondering about the meaning and purpose of my own life.

After a day of hard work, I needed the rest, and sleep took over me and my thoughts.

ONE EVENING, later in the week, I was sitting alone in the small garden in our home and taking my evening tea. The roses were in full bloom, and a light breeze was spreading their delicate fragrance all around. It was the weekend and I did not have to go to the clinic next day. In that moment of quiet relaxation, my thoughts went back to my childhood memories and my past experiences.

My mother gave me the name, Aparna. I had the good fortune of taking birth in a well-to-do family in India, and receiving the best education both in my home country as well as in England and America, that led to a professional qualification in medicine. I returned to India and started practicing as a gynecologist and child specialist. I have been doing this for 12 years in a renowned hospital in the country. Fortunately, I have been able to build a very good reputation for myself as a medical doctor in the field of my specialization.

I come from an orthodox religious family and I believe in God – or a Supreme Divine Power, but I do not completely fit into any religious category. Due to my family background, and the influence of my grandparents at my early age, I had more than average exposure to religion and spirituality. However, my own spiritual orientation is self-discovered, and not taught by any religious denomination. I also realize that even after having achieved a high level of education and professional success as measured by socially accepted parameters, I am still searching for meaning and purpose of my life.

In fact, I am trying to find my own self. I seem to know what I am not, but I have yet to discover who I am. I do not know exactly in what direction my life will move, or where I may find my answers. A feeling inside tells me that the direction will lead to the spiritual domain, toward the search for a divine power, and for my own spiritual self that in some way is connected to that power.

As I look at myself, my spiritual awareness appears to have two dimensions – external and internal. The most obvious one is linked to my external connections with the community and my work for some religious and charitable institutions run by some very noble and devoted persons. I see their faith in God, and I try to understand the scriptures and the lovely routines of worship in various forms, which seem to have a profound effect of uplifting the spirit and cleansing the mind. As I see it, this is the external face of my inner spiritual self.

On the other hand, deep inside my heart, my private urge is one of inner spiritual search. On the outside, I say traditional prayers to God which are heartfelt and genuine. But in my private meditation, I delve back in time, beyond the confines of the temples, institutions and holy places. I try to look back to the Creator, to the source of all life, to the reality of my own self, and the divine power manifesting itself everywhere.

I search for the meaning of life, and I feel frustrated to see lives being spent and wasted away in all the conflict, confrontation and consequent unhappiness in the world. I wish to draw upon divine love and power to help me achieve my true potential in life. I want to understand and accept the path chosen for me. I want to make myself a better person, and I want to live constantly in the presence of the divine.

Every day, I try to step temporarily out of my routine and mundane work and find some quiet time when I can meditate. This can be anywhere at any time. Sometimes, even at work, I take out a few minutes, close my eyes and go 'inward' into my own inner center, free from the distractions of daily life. I often seek the calming effect of meditation if the day has been stressful, or just a moment to touch the spirit within, to find some comfort in the middle of a rather maddening world.

Sitting in my peaceful garden, I realize that I need guidance and help to move on to the right path without losing much time. Time just seems to be slipping away, and in the middle of my hectic and busy life, days and months keep passing away too fast. Only my hope gives me a positive outlook for the future.

Indeed, at times of great stress or sadness, I have been fortunate to have experienced spiritual cleansing and empowerment in the form of some light that enters my body and gives me inner calm and peace. Such experiences help me face the future with a positive outlook. But I need to understand fully and clearly the reality of my own self, the fundamental basis which connects me to the divine force, the processes which make it work, and how I can channel these in the desired direction.

Coming from my exposure to the modern western world of

science and technology, and my own professional background, I often wonder whether all that scientific knowledge and experience, which have been so successful in the material world, can contribute to this search for meaning, purpose and spirituality in my life. I continue to carry a rather uncomfortable feeling of being divided between my spiritual self on the one hand, and my worldly existence on the other, and the consequent contradiction in my own life as I live day to day in this world.[1]

My husband, Raj is very supportive. He is a distinguished lawyer, quite successful and therefore quite busy. He reads a lot, about anything and everything, and I often wonder how he manages to find time for that. He encourages me to read as well, and that has taken me to the literature on religion and philosophy. He has a rather keen sense of observation, and understands me and my thoughts.

He had just returned by a late night flight after a rather hectic day of meetings, and I too had quite a stressful day at the hospital due to a very complicated delivery case. As we started talking, rather abruptly, I said: "Raj, I don't want to continue like this, I am seriously thinking of leaving the hospital. I need to focus on myself, and I wish to spend some time at an Ashram in Rishikesh, to get some peace, learn yoga and meditation in a proper way, and find out what I have been searching for all these years. I have heard a lot about Parmarth Ashram, and some very learned and enlightened saints there, and I want to go there."

Raj did not say no, but jokingly asked: "That sounds like a great idea. Will you take me with you? I do not want to be left behind."

I replied: "Yes, if you can get out of your never-ending

work and keep your clients away for a while, all of which I seriously doubt whether you can do, now or ever. This has become your life, you seem to value that, and I don't know if you would want anything else."

He just shook his head and laughed. But, I must say, due to his genuine support for me, within three weeks I found myself in Rishikesh.

THIS IS THE PLACE where the holy river Ganges comes down from the mountains and enters the plains, its waters rushing forward in full glory. All the surroundings are blessed with great natural beauty. The spiritual atmosphere and serenity of the place provide a feeling of heavenly peace and calm, which spontaneously influence the mind to think and contemplate. There is a beautiful Ashram, known as Parmarth Niketan, right on the bank of the holy river. The Ashram is looked after by a very intelligent, enlightened and dedicated young saint, Swami Chidanand. I found it a lovely place.

When I reached the Ashram, I was somewhat pleasantly surprised that besides the holy saints in their saffron clothing, some truly dedicated and highly educated persons were living full time and running some very good programs at the Ashram. These included a well-equipped yoga and meditation centre, a nature cure hospital, and an educational school for children and young students. In addition to a regular syllabus, the school very well covered subjects of religion and culture.

Apart from the temples and places of worship, the Ashram had a fine music academy which was run by a lovely lady, Maa Amrita. Before coming to the Ashram about six years ago, she managed a highly prestigious public school. She had acquired deep knowledge of yoga and meditation and was managing the Yoga and Meditation centre at the Ashram. Being an accomplished singer with a melodious voice, she was also regularly singing devotional music at the evening program of prayers on the bank of the holy river Ganges every day, and also for festivals and other important functions in the Ashram.

My first day at the Ashram started with a meeting with Maa Amrita at 5am before sunrise, when morning yoga and meditation class started. The program began with the chanting of the Gayatri Mantra. This is a most sacred ancient mantra dedicated to the invocation of Sun as the divine source of all energy which permeates the entire living world. This was followed by an elaborate sequence of yogic exercises, breathing and Pranayama, and finally meditation. It transformed my entire system and I felt a relaxed and heightened awareness of my body and mind in a state of peace and calm.

After the class was over, Maa Amrita sat down to talk to me, and asked me what I was looking for.

Trying to be as focused as possible, I said: "Maa, I am a successful medical doctor and have no complaints about my career and work, but I still do not know, why I am doing all this, and where it is going to take me. I have three questions for which I am trying to find answers. One, who am I? Two, what is this world – is it real, or is it just an illusion or Maya? And three, how do I fit into this world – as an individual, and with others."

She looked at me with a smile, but kept quiet.

And then I added: "Maa, these are not just abstract or philosophical questions for me. I think these have very practical relevance to my own life. As I live from day-to-day trying to do my best as a medical doctor, I see so much suffering all over not only with my patients and children who come to me, but with so many others everywhere. I really do not understand why there is so much conflict and unhappiness all around."

Maa laughed and said: "You are so highly educated, successful and smart, and you probably know that more than two-and-half centuries ago, Gautam Buddha asked similar questions. Don't you know, and accept his answers?"

I replied with some hesitation: "Yes, he got the enlightenment, but I am not Gautam Buddha. I need my own answers." She kept quiet, and waited for me to continue.

I continued: "Maa, I am educated and trained in the western world in medical science, and as a medical doctor, I work for results and look for prevention and cure of ailments. These results must be actually seen and proven on a scientific basis. I do not know if the answers to my questions can be found on a similar scientific basis. I have great respect for religion, ethics and moral principles, and these have surely attempted to give the answers, but these do not seem to work in real life. The world goes on with conflict, war, fear, insecurity, lust and greed – instead of peace, harmony, love, compassion and kindness. This is evident both at our individual personal level and our collective social level. In such a situation, what do we do?"

Maa asked: "Why do you say that? Don't you see peace and harmony anywhere?"

I hesitated, but said: "Everyone wants it, but no one finds it. There must be a reason for that. But I do not know."

Maa was quiet for few moments, and then said something that surprised me: "What is your address?"

"Why?" I asked, and added: "I live in my house in Delhi, in Panchsheel Park. But why are you asking?"

"Just want to know, where to find you, if I want." She continued: "But as I understand, your body lives there, and as you know, you are not your body. So, where do you live?"

I thought for a moment, and replied: "OK, I see. Then, I would say, I live in my body. Does that answer your question?"

Maa looked at me intently, and then said: "Need to know where to find 'you' and not just your body. If you are searching for something, it helps to know where you expect to find it. You are searching for your own self, are you not? So, you should try to know where you can expect to find it. If it is inside, is there any point in searching for it outside? Is that what you have been doing?"

I kept quiet. And Maa went on.

She said: "Obviously, you have a nice house in Delhi and you take great care of it. Do you do the same for your body in which you said you live? Do you even know your body and understand it well?"

This was an easy question for me, and I was quick to reply: "Maa, I am a medical doctor and deal with bodies all the time. I understand the strengths, weaknesses, and problems of human bodies. That is a doctor's work, and I think I do that well."

Maa said: "I am not talking about human bodies in general. I am talking about your body, the body which you say you live in. What about that?"

"OK." I said: "I know my body. I am 5 feet 3 inches tall, have a fair complexion, dark brown hair, and…"

She interrupted: "No need to tell that, anyone can see all that appears outside. But you say you live inside. Do you know the force at work inside your body, the force which drives it, or the energy that makes it work?"

I could give a good lecture on this, but held back.

I replied: "Yes, we learn this as part of our medical education and training. I know that my body consists of over one trillion cells, and each organ is made up of cells specific to that particular organ. I also know that my entire biological system is connected by a network of arteries and veins through which blood flows and carries oxygen and a variety of nutrients to the cells to give them the power to keep working."

I was not sure whether she wanted to hear all this. But she was listening attentively.

So, I continued: "Maa, let me also tell you that each single cell in our body is designed to perform the processes that sustain life. It is an amazing fact that these body cells are being constantly renewed and replaced as a natural ongoing process. I understand that over one hundred thousand cells in a human body are eliminated and replaced by new cells every minute. So, while I am sitting here before you, right now my old cells are being replaced by new cells. If these cells or their functions become distorted or damaged for any reason, our medical science is supposed to remedy the situation to support and correct this process. This is part of my job as a doctor."

Maa said: "You are a very good doctor to explain all this to me. But you should also tell me what empowers and drives this process which continues non-stop from birth to death."

"I really do not know, but I understand that there is some kind of energy flowing through my body." I added: "I think when the energy flow emerges, life begins, and when it ceases, life ends, and that is what we call birth and death. If the flow of energy becomes blocked or obstructed, problems arise in the body and its organs."

"That is a very intelligent way to look at it." Maa said, and then asked: "But where does this energy come from in the first place, and how does it continue to flow thereafter?"

"Maa, I can tell you only what I have learned, and as you know, I am not a student of physics." I said.

After a brief pause, I added: "All I know is that science understands such energy as force acting upon matter. This force works not only within our body but everywhere, including our earth, other planets and stars, and matter in all its forms. In this context, classical science has found that matter consists of molecules, which consist of atoms, which in turn are made up of a nucleus of protons and neutrons in the center of an atom and surrounded by electrons orbiting around the nucleus. These are understood as the smallest possible constituents of matter, and are often described as particles."

Maa was listening attentively.

So, I continued: "The known forces recognized by science as working upon matter are –strong and weak nuclear forces, which work at the level of atoms and electrons; electrical and magnetic forces, which are now considered together as electro-magnetic force; and gravitational force, which works as a force attracting matter having a mass. I think, since the time of the great scientist Albert Einstein, there have been attempts to find one unified force, but that effort is still continuing. In the meantime, during the last century, there have been far-reaching developments in quantum physics, which have now found that beyond the particles and everything else, it is quantum energy that is at work."

"Yes, I have also heard about quantum physics, and that sounds very interesting." Maa said: "And do you see any bearing of these developments in quantum physics in relation to your own self and your own body?"

I did not consider myself competent enough to try to explain quantum physics to such an enlightened person sitting in front of me. And it was even more difficult when she had asked about its relevance to my own self and body.

I thought it best to refer her to someone who had done pioneering work on this subject, and I said: "Maa, I have with me two books from a renowned author Fritjof Capra, titled 'Uncommon Wisdom' and 'The Web of Life' which can give you an idea of the current thinking on this subject. I will leave these books with you, if you can find time to take a look at them."[2]

She said, yes, with a smile. Much later I found out she had already read not only these two books, but almost every other book on the subject, written by many famous authors.

A little later, when I delivered the two books, Maa gave me a book titled 'Vivek Chudamani'. This was written by Aadi Guru Shankaracharya, in the 8th century and continues to be regarded as an authoritative interpretation and commentary on Advaita Vedanta philosophy in India since ancient times. I knew this book was being given to me as my homework, before we met again.[3]

My meeting with Maa Amrita that morning left me with a new sense of awareness and direction in which my search was going to move forward.

AFTER A LIGHT VEGETARIAN lunch and some rest, I met another intelligent woman in the Ashram. Her name was Dr. Sonali. She was born and brought up in England, and then she moved to America and qualified there as a medical doctor specializing in child psychology. Later, I learned that she also had been a faculty member at the San Francisco Medical Research Center in California.

She had come to the Ashram five years ago, and was devoting her time to managing the medical facilities provided at the Ashram free of charge to the public, and to organize medical relief camps regularly held at the Ashram and also at nearby places in the mountains. Thousands of people came to these camps to receive free medical help and treatments for child health, eye care, maternity welfare, and preventive medicine for cardiac and respiratory ailments. I discovered that some of the best doctors in the country were regularly coming to these camps every year to provide their services free of charge. All this was happening at the initiative and inspiration being given by the spiritual leader who was presiding over the affairs of the Ashram.

When I met Dr. Sonali, she was dressed in a simple white gown that covered her from shoulders to feet. Her voice and manner carried an obvious authoritative imprint which came most probably from her long stay and education in America.

I had an instant communication with her as we both shared the same professional background in medicine. She was quite enthusiastic in giving me the details of the charitable work and services she was organizing under the banner of the Ashram. She was also curious to know what had brought me to the Ashram.

I briefly mentioned to her about the discussions I had at

my morning meeting with Maa. She was not surprised to hear that I was interested in exploring the energy flows within my body as understood from a spiritual perspective.

"I have been working on this subject for many years." She said, smiling: "I have also set up some very good equipment for identifying and testing the human energy field we call human aura. We are now able to do online recording of bio-feedback and human aura. We have used this equipment for medical diagnostic purposes as well as for choosing alternate-medicine treatments for ailments like asthma, arthritis, blood pressure, diabetics, and insomnia. The results have been quite good."

She continued: "These energy based treatments fit in very well with the herbal therapies of our ancient Indian medical system of Ayurveda, the chromo-therapy and aroma-therapy, and the yoga and meditation programs we run at Yoga and Nature Cure Center in the Ashram."

I very much wanted to see the equipment set up by her, and to know how it worked. She took me for a quick tour to see the Yoga and Nature Cure Center, and the bio-feedback and aura related equipments which were installed in a separate section.

The equipment for aura reading and analysis was made by a German company known as Aura Med Gmbh and this was developed on the basis of research work done over a number of years by a German lady Martina Gruber, and her team of software and electronic engineers. Sonali told me the equipment had been certified for medical diagnostic purposes in 28 countries. It had a flat panel, and under the panel, there were electrodes connected to the main control panel. The processing in the control panel was done by a set of software programs also developed by the same team.

"Would you like me to take a reading of your energy field and aura?" She asked me.

I readily said, yes.

I was asked to place my hand for a few seconds on a panel, at the right position. The information of energy flowing in my body was electronically picked up by the electrodes under the panel, and this was instantly transmitted to the main control panel. The software in the system then analyzed the information, and displayed an image of my aura. It was quite fascinating to see my own aura on the screen.

Sonali pointed out that this image was automatically color-coded by the system, and the picture on the screen showed aura around different parts of my body in different colors and shades such as purple, blue, green, yellow, red, and white. These colors and shades represented different light frequencies of aura at different parts of my body. She also pointed out some places in my aura image where the energy flow seemed to be weaker or was getting blocked; and these indicated some problem at those points.

She then switched the equipment to show the analysis done by the software in the system. This was most interesting, and showed how my seven chakras were working, and also how my various body organs and systems were functioning at that time. The software was programmed to show the working of heart, lungs, kidneys, spleen, and other organs in the body – 42 organs in all. Sonali told me that these results could be cross-checked with the clinical examination of the related body part, and in most cases these matched very well. In many cases, these were also able to predict and give advance warning about an impending ailment or problem likely to arise in the body.

Based upon these results, an intelligent choice could be made for the most appropriate therapy to be used in each case.

Here I saw a very good illustration and some independently verifiable evidence of energy field in the human body, and its connectivity to the functioning of the various organs and systems within the body. Being a medical doctor, I found it very interesting that the human body could be understood and examined on the principle of an energy field, and this could be done on an objectively verifiable basis with the help of such equipment.

Sonali gave me the print-outs for my aura and energy field, and also the chart showing the working of various organs based upon the analysis of my energy field. This reminded me of the equipments we use in our medical practice, for electro-cardiogram (ECG) reports showing the working of heart, electro-encephalograph (EEG) showing the mapping of brain, and many others, which pick up information from human body and provide a diagnostic report. But until now, I had never realized that we could also tap into the human energy field and get information about the working of the body based upon energy flowing in it.

While handing over these print outs, Sonali told me: "You must know that the aura keeps changing as the level and flow of energy in the body changes. So, if you take a reading of your aura at another time, it would show a different picture if your energy field has changed."

"This is very interesting." She added: "This means that you can take a reading before undergoing a therapy, or before doing yoga and meditation, and then you can take another reading after that; and you can then see the difference made in your body by the particular therapy, or yoga or meditation program."

I could see that the results of these therapies and programs could then be understood and evaluated objectively, and not just on a subjective feeling or judgment of a person. This was indeed a great step toward development of knowledge in this field.

We then sat down to talk over a cup of tea in the lounge at the Yoga Center. I was keen to know more about human energy field.

I asked her: "Sonali, your equipment, software, and the reports generated, are indeed very fascinating. I am now wondering if this concept of human energy is recognized in modern science, and whether this is also accepted in the spiritual world."

She replied: "Yes, it is a long story, and it is being accepted now. This is because both science and spirituality now recognize energy as the basic reality underlying everything. The developments in science in the field of quantum physics have indeed brought science much closer to spirituality than ever before. If you are really interested in this subject, and if you have the time, let me show you a short audio–visual presentation we have prepared at the Ashram on this subject."

I could not say no, and we settled down to watch this presentation on the TV monitor in the lounge. This presentation started with a picture of the sun rising. The commentary continued with visuals changing in step with it.

"Whenever we think of energy, the first thought goes to sun as the source of energy, which flows as light, heat, and radiation in various forms. The sun looks so beautiful and energizing at sunrise and sunset, and is seen in full glory at mid-day. But a closer look would show that it is a huge ball of fire with enormous heat and radiation flowing from it.

This energy flowing down to earth is considered to be the source of all life on earth, in all forms. This energy shows up in nature everywhere. For example, we can see it in the movement of water – like sea waves; in the flow of air – like breeze, storms and hurricanes; in the radiation of heat – like fire; and in the field of light – like sunlight and moonlight. All of these energy-driven phenomena support life at various levels in the world of human beings, animals and plants."

The presentation and commentary continued.

"Science has understood these energy flows as forces, and has described them in four categories. Sir Isaac Newton, the great scientist in 16th century, saw an apple falling from the tree, and discovered the force of gravitation as the force which attracts two objects having a mass; and that force accounts for the movement of objects in relation to each other. He found that the planets in the solar system which move in their orbits around the sun are also driven by the same energy, now known as gravitational force."

"Later, George Maxwell, another great scientist in the 17th century, studied the electrical and magnetic forces which arise from the flow of electrons within a system, and he showed that these are interlinked. These were then together known as electro-magnetic force, which is considered to be the most powerful force responsible for movements in the world of matter."

"Albert Einstein, the greatest scientist in the world of physics, studied the structure of atom and showed the relationship of energy and matter in his famous equation $E=mc^2$. He explained the nuclear forces operating in matter at the atomic level, and showed that a strong nuclear force held the nucleus together, and a weak nuclear force held the electrons in their orbits around the nucleus."

"As a result of these discoveries, the forces known to science are grouped in four categories: strong nuclear force, weak nuclear force, electro-magnetic force, and gravitational force. These forces act upon matter and that explains the working of everything on earth, as well as in the solar system – including the movement of planets in their orbits around the sun. Molecules, atoms and particles are the building blocks which make up the matter that we see around us. Different structure and properties of matter result from the structure and arrangement of these building blocks in a variety of permutation and combinations. This is the position in classical physics as developed over several centuries of scientific studies and research."

The presentation then switched to another sequence of visuals, as the commentary continued.

"Early in the 20th century, quantum physics discovered that particles which were until then considered to be the smallest constituents of matter, were themselves not solid material substance, but had to be understood in terms of quantum energy and not as matter. The earlier view had seen matter – and forces acting upon matter – as two separate things. Even though Einstein had shown the equivalence relationship between energy and matter having mass, these were accepted as two separate realities. Quantum physics showed a different position."

"As per the new developments in quantum physics, the smallest conceivable bit of energy was called quanta, and this was at work at the sub-atomic level, that is, at the level below the structure of neutron, protons, and other known particles which make up the atom. It was in the 1920s when Max Planck also discovered that energy radiation was not continuous, but in packets of energy, he called quanta."

"It was later found by other scientists, including Neil Bohr, Werner Heisenberg and Erwin Schrodinger that it was this quantum energy that was working everywhere, and connected everything at the quantum level. Accordingly, one way to understand a quanta is to visualize it as a pulsating and vibrating smallest conceivable bit of energy, which is at the root of everything at the most fundamental sub-atomic level."[4]

I was finding this most interesting. Until then, I had only a vague idea about the concept of quantum energy. I was now discovering its true meaning and significance. The audio-visual continued and I kept watching it with full attention.

"These developments in quantum physics are based upon rigorous and repeated scientific studies and experiments, and the discoveries have introduced far-reaching and revolutionary changes in the scientific understanding of the world and its working."

"These new discoveries in quantum physics include the following:[5]

One: A particle has wave-particle duality, which means that the same particle can behave as a particle of matter at one time and as a wave of energy at another time, and it all depends upon the context of the experiment and observation. This shows that the classical distinction between matter and energy and their separate behaviors and consequences, is not valid at the fundamental quantum level of reality.

Two: At the quantum level, all potential states of energy and matter co-exist until the event takes place, and any one of them can be crystallized as observed reality, again depending upon the context. This is described as quantum indeterminacy.

Three: All particles are inter-connected at the quantum level. Since these particles are the basic constituents of everything, this means that everything in the world is interconnected at the fundamental level, and therefore, everything affects everything else at that level. This is called quantum interconnectivity."

"Taking a cue from the development of quantum physics, the energy flowing inside the human body may also be seen and understood in terms of quantum energy. Every cell in the human body, which consists of molecules, atoms and particles, is basically made up of quantum energy, and therefore, has all the three quantum characteristics mentioned above."

"In simple terms, this implies that all human beings are bundles of quantum energy, which is constantly pulsating and vibrating. Recent research has now shown that each cell in the human body is vibrating at more than a million vibrations per second. Research has also shown that all the resulting forces within our body, including the positive and negative forces, are in a state of complete balance, and therefore, we do not feel their enormous pull. These positive and negative forces within the human body arise from the positive polarity of a proton and the negative polarity of an electron within each atom in the body. This is indeed a marvel of nature that has programmed the human body and its systems in such a perfect equilibrium. If this was disturbed, there would be disastrous consequences for our survival. For example, it has been calculated that if there were one percent more electrons than protons, beyond their normal numbers in the human body, then the resulting force at an arm's length would be so strong as to lift not only the Empire State building in New York, not only the Mount Everest in the Himalayas, but strong enough to lift the entire earth!"[6]

After showing these energy forces as understood in the

field of science, the audio-visual presentation then proceeded to show the corresponding understanding of energy in the ancient Indian knowledge of Vedanta and related scriptures.

This part showed an outline of a human figure surrounded by light radiating on all sides. The light was bright just outside the body and became softer as it spread out, and this showed a projection of human aura emanating from the body. It then showed three main pathways of energy flowing inside the body, which were called Naadis, meaning meridians or channels of flow. These were named as Ida, Pingla and Sushamna, each of these starting at the root of the spine, and going up around the vertebra all the way to the back of the head. Energy appearing as pulsating light was flowing in each of these three pathways. It was interesting to note that the energy flow in Ida was clockwise, while the energy flow in Pingla was counter-clockwise, and both these were entwined around the central Naadi called Sushamna.

Sonali explained how energy flowing in such a pattern creates a field, and in the case of electrical energy in motion, this would appear as an electro-magnetic field. She said that the human energy field was similar to an electro-magnetic field.

The audio-visual then showed the system which was regulating the energy flow inside the human body. It showed the Naadis, or channels or meridians, in which the energy flows. Sonali told me that there are believed to be over 84,000 such Naadis in a human body, and there are seven Chakras which work as energy centers. Since these centers are constantly spinning, these are termed as Chakras, which literally means spinning wheels. Interestingly, each Chakra is linked to a particular element making up the body. [7]

The presentation showed that when all of the Chakras are

Human Energy Field and Chakras

fully energized and function in equilibrium, all the connected elements working within the human body – earth, water, fire, air, sound and light – maintain balance and harmony. Each Chakra can be awakened and fully energized when the dormant energy called Kundalini, lying at the base of the spine, is awakened and starts moving up from one Chakra to the next. This process of awakening of Kundalini and activating all the Chakras is made possible by appropriate yoga techniques, which are described in the ancient scriptures.

I watched the presentation with full attention and found it very interesting. I had earlier read about Chakras and Naadis, but after seeing the presentation, I realized that my knowledge had been quite sketchy and superficial.

Since Sonali seemed to know the subject so well, I asked her two questions: "Sonali, you know so much about this subject. Can you help me understand two things?

One: Has any one done experimental work to find out if Chakras and Naadis really exist and work in our body?

Two: If we do have such a system working in our body, what is the force that makes it work? Is it the same as electrical force, and does it create an electro-magnetic field as your presentation says?"

"Aparna, you are indeed a difficult person to satisfy." She added, laughing: "But I like your questions. We can spend the whole day discussing these, but I will briefly tell you what I know."

"To answer your first question, let me say that a lot of work has been done on Chakras and Naadis by many research scholars, and many books have been written on this subject.. Some of the names which readily come to mind are: Hiroshi Motoyama, Charles W. Leadbeater, Michael Talbot,

Dr. William Collinge, Shalila Sharamon and Bodo J. Bagniski. We have their books in our library, and you can take them to read, if you like. The one I like best is from Hiroshi Motoyama."[8]

I was keen to know the result of their work.

I asked Sonali: "Can you tell me about the work done by Motoyama?"

She was quite happy to see my interest in the subject, and told me: "Motoyama and his team of researchers conducted extensive experiments at the Institute of Religion and Psychology in Japan and found substantial electro-physiological evidence for the existence of Chakras and Naadis and the energy flowing through them. These experiments and their conclusions have been described in detail in his book 'Theories of Chakras – Bridge to Higher Consciousness'. These experiments have been conducted under controlled conditions with specially devised electro-magnetic instruments for measuring radiations from human body at specific points. The resulting data has been utilized for analyzing energy flows through Naadis or meridians and Chakras."

With my background as a medical doctor, I was curious to know if we could do anything to influence or stimulate a Chakra working inside the human body, and I asked Sonali if Motoyama's experiments had found anything to show this.

She convincingly answered: "Yes. These experiments also monitored electrical field vibrations of specific Chakras like Anahata Chakra and Manipura Chakra, and studied their co-relation with certain yogic techniques of concentration and relaxation which were able to modulate or intensify those vibrations. This means that we can actually improve the working of a Chakra by these yogic techniques."

She added: "Motoyama also investigated the activation or awakening of Chakras. In his book, he narrates his own experience of successive awakening of his Chakras over a period, and that makes fascinating reading. In all, his experiments covered over 2,000 subjects."

This information was most convincing for me.

Sonali had anticipated my query about the scientific instruments used by Motoyama for conducting these experiments.

She helpfully added: "One of the instruments designed and used by Motoyama for this purpose is known as A.M.I – an acronym for 'Apparatus for Meridian Identification.' This is a very sensitive electro-magnetic monitoring device that measures the flow of ions through tissue layers below the skin surface. The patterns of flowing streams of ions show the channels of energy flow in the body."

"Are there others who have also found similar results?" I asked.

She was ready with the answer, and said: "Motoyama's research and conclusions regarding human energy field have been recognized and confirmed by many others. They have identified light emission from Chakras as 'photons' and have recognized this as scientific evidence for the energy field of human body."

"Sonali, can you tell me more about the work done by others?" I persisted.

She was amused at my curiosity, and responded with a smile.

She said: "Aparna, I know you won't leave me until I answer all your questions. Yes, there are many others who have done interesting work and got similar results. For instance,

Dr. Valerie Hunt at the University of California in Los Angeles derived similar results by using electromyography. By placing electrodes upon the skin surface, she found regular, high frequency signals from the Chakra points. The more active a Chakra was, the more the photons it emitted. This has been verified in laboratory studies with subjects doing meditation in a darkened room."

She looked at me as I was listening with full attention.

She continued: "Further research by others also has shown the existence of an energy field around the human body. This has been described by different names like aura or bio-field. An interesting example of this work is the research conducted at Yale University by a team headed by Dr. HS Burr and Dr. FSC Northrop. They conducted a series of experiments to determine the validity of their 'electro-dynamic' theory of life. Their experiments showed that all living things had a complex electrical field surrounding them that extended beyond the limits of human vision. They used an extremely sensitive device – an ultra-sensitive micro-voltmeter, which was capable of measuring these electrical fields down to a millionth of a volt. They found that not only did such a field exist around a living organism, but as oxygen was removed from its environment, the surrounding electrical field began to contract without changing its overall shape; and it disappeared at the moment of death. If you are interested, you can read about these experiments in Joseph Ostrom's book 'Understanding Auras'.[9]

I was trying to quietly absorb what Sonali had told me. My mind visualized the picture of an energy field around the human body. I was also reminded of the notion of human 'aura' that was believed to be something like a halo or light radiating from the human body. Many a time, pictures of deities or highly-evolved saints showed such a halo around their heads. I asked Sonali whether aura was also some kind of an energy field.

She was quite willing to explain, and said: "The notion of aura has been recognized in our ancient literature and also by modern writers. Aura is seen as light emanating from the human body and forming an energy field around it. Kirlian photography provides visual photographic depiction of human aura by capturing the energy radiation on photographic paper. This technique was invented by a Russian scientist Semyorn Kirlian, and is therefore so named. The equipment usually consists of bio-feedback sensors held by a person in his hands, a computer, and a special camera or video-recorder. This captures on a photographic film the person's electro-magnetic field which is seen as the aura."

She paused for a while, and then added: "Some others like Dr. William Collinge prefer to call this a 'bio-field' instead of aura. Dr. Pavek at the Biofield Research Institute in Sausalito, California, also called this 'bio-field' and viewed it as the energy field that must be present for life to exist."

After this long and comprehensive description, Sonali asked me if I was tired; but I wanted to continue. She got up and made two cups of coffee for us.

She then continued: "As for your second question, there is now adequate research to show that electro-magnetic forces run and control practically the entire body system. From the smallest cell to the most vital organs in the body, electrical force is the driving force. The enormous magnitude of the electrical force within the human body is not readily felt by us because of the extremely fine balance maintained between positive and negative charges. Our biological electrical circuits run on a very minute scale. These circuits are miniaturized beyond the dreams of any micro-chip designer."

I was not sure whether I fully understood what she had said. I wanted to explore further.

I asked: "Sonali, although I am a medical doctor, this is becoming too technical for me to follow. Can you elaborate with some example to help me better understand this?"

She paused for a moment, and then said: "OK. Let me give you an example. At the level of a cell, these electrical charges are separated by the thickness of a membrane – about five nanometers, or less than a millionth of the width of a fingernail. The voltages are equally tiny – about 0.1 volts. However, 0.1 volts across a five nanometer membrane equals an electrical field of 20 million volts per meter. Just to give you an idea of how strong this is I may point out that the electrical field in the lightening in a thunder-storm is about one million volts per meter. This means that our electrical field is almost 20 times stronger than the electrical field of lightening in a thunderstorm! So, you can imagine the enormous electrical power which is at work within our bodies."[10]

I was not only over-awed with this information, but was also greatly impressed by the deep knowledge of Sonali on the subject. Obviously, this was acquired by her from her own study and research. I looked at her with deep appreciation in my eyes.

She continued: "Let me also tell you that at the level of molecules which make up our body, the electrical force becomes quite strong, since the mass of molecules is very small, and the strength of the force increases inversely with the square of distance. We do not realize that almost all movements of our muscles and nerve cells are driven by electrical force working within our body; and all these happen as a response to changes in the voltage difference across cell membranes."[11]

"Can you again help me with some examples?" I asked.

She smiled and said: "You probably know about this as much as I do. But, let me give you a few interesting examples. The brain functions provide a marvelous example of a fully integrated electrical and chemical process within our body. You probably already know that our brain has about 100 billion neurons, which are minute extended cells and form a delicate and extensive network. This is the network through which the transmission of information in our brain takes place as a combined electrical and chemical process. As you know, nerve impulses pass across neurons as electrical signals, which then release chemical neuro-transmitters to link with other neurons."

She found me listening with full attention, and continued: "Example of our heart is even more interesting. Our heart also works on electro-magnetic energy. Each heartbeat creates a wave of electro-magnetic force that moves out and creates an electro-magnetic field. Researchers have found that in terms of electro-magnetic power, the heart produces about 2.5 watts with each beat – enough to power a night-light or a small radio! The amplitude of the electric wave produced by the beating heart is about 50 times that of our brain waves, and the heart's magnetic field is about a thousand times stronger than that of the brain. It is also interesting to know that our heart signal does not stop at the skin but radiates into the space around us. The electro-magnetic field of heart can actually be detected by a magnetometer four or five feet away from the heart."[12]

It was fascinating to listen to Sonali and I was most impressed with her knowledge.

I told her: "You have more than answered my questions. I really want to thank you for your wonderful audio-visual presentation about the human energy field. It is indeed a beautiful presentation and has given me a good understanding of human energy field, and the energy flowing through my own body."

Sonali replied: "Yes, the purpose of this presentation was to show the energy flowing through the human body, and how it shows up as a human energy field within which the entire human body exists and functions. I am very happy that you found it interesting."

I said: "Sonali, this has been very helpful for me. I now need to think more to understand the relationship between my body and my energy field."

She smiled and said: "That is quite evident. Let me put it this way – our body and its systems become active when the energy field emerges, and become defunct when the energy field regresses. Its emergence is birth and its regression is death. If you understand this, you realize that this human energy field is the ground for our existence, and for our consciousness."

I could not help asking: "Sonali, is this just a scientific view point, or is this also shared by our scriptures?"

She was quite enthusiastic with her answer, and said: "This is a very important question you have asked. Let me tell you that in our ancient scriptures, this energy field is understood as the 'soul'. As you know, usually, soul is considered to be a meta-physical and spiritual power, but this interpretation of soul as an energy field gives it a scientific meaning, and this can be easily understood in a way as we understand an electro-magnetic field, or more accurately, a quantum energy field. In a very significant way, this interpretation beautifully unifies the concept of energy field in science and the concept of soul in spirituality."

It was obvious that Sonali had done deep study on this subject.

I asked her: "Sonali, I have one more question. Can you please also explain how this unified concept can help me in understanding the identity of my own self and my connectivity to the Supreme Divine from a spiritual perspective?"

She looked at me intently, and after a little pause, said: "Our Swami Ji is going to speak tomorrow morning on the subject of our divine self. I suggest you attend this session, which will be in the main lecture hall, at 9am. I think it will be useful for you to hear him."

We had been together for more than two hours, and Sonali pointed out that it was time for the evening Aarti prayer ceremony and we should join that program.

The Ashram holds a wonderful program of Aarti every evening on the Ashram steps going down to the river. Aarti is offered as a daily prayer to the holy Ganges, with Vedic chanting, devotional music, and lighting of lamps. Thousands of persons join this program everyday, and it is quite a moving experience. One sits on the steps, looking at the holy river flowing by, against a backdrop of the Himalayas and the evening sun beyond. It is a beautiful view as the setting sun sends down cascades of amber light which shine on the waters of the river in a most glorious way.

We walked up to the platform on the bank of the river. It was already full of people who had come to participate in the ceremony. Sonali arranged to have me seated comfortably at a place where I could watch the entire program, and then left to attend to her part of the work at this ceremony.

The river Ganges had a mighty current flowing down, and the water was crystal clear, as this was the place where it had just come out of the mountains and entered the plains. As I sat on the platform, the river was flowing in front of me, and beyond the other bank of river, there was a mountain range, and beyond that the sun was slowly descending for sunset. The sunlight was changing the color of the clouds to shades of saffron, and the entire sky above and beyond was transformed into a most beautiful play of light and its changing shades. This beautiful view, and the vast expanse and lovely sound of flowing water, were giving me a delightful experience of sight and sound.

I was simply overwhelmed, absorbing this wonderful sight and experience. Quietly, I closed my eyes and all my awareness came into sharp focus. With my eyes closed, and sitting on the bank of the holy river, I had the most pleasant sensation of feeling a cool breeze touching my body, hearing the musical sound of the flowing water, and experiencing the glow of the evening sunlight on my face. In that moment, I had a feeling of bliss, which was as close to an eternal bliss as I could imagine.

In the next few minutes, the Aarti program started with a chanting of Vedic mantras by students from the school run by the Ashram. This was accompanied by a Yagna ceremony, which meant lighting of the holy fire and offering some specially prepared edible matter into it. The fragrance of the burning matter in the holy fire filled up the atmosphere and purified the entire place.

Maa Amrita sang two devotional songs in her melodious voice, which transformed the place as if all of us were sitting inside a holy temple in the presence of some divine power. One devotional song was to welcome and praise the holy river

Ganges, as the divine mother which has come down from the heavens to wash away sins of all people on earth, and give them peace and prosperity. The other song was for the invocation of the supreme lord and his powers for the good of everyone, everywhere, and to remind us of the sacred principle that the whole world is one family and all places are places of God.

I had heard these before, but it was the first time that I found myself so emotional and so sensitive to these thoughts and feelings. The Aarti ceremony concluded with the lighting of hundreds of oil lamps and candles and offering them with prayers in praise of the mother Ganges. That beautiful sight of hundreds of lighted lamps and candles swinging in the hands of devotees and their reflections in the flowing waters of the holy river, was an unforgettable sight, and has remained fresh in my memory.

I slept very peacefully that night.

THE NEXT MORNING, I was in the lecture hall to hear Swami Ji. He was the one who was leading and coordinating the affairs of the Ashram. In his own right, he was a highly evolved saint and was greatly revered in the spiritual field in the country. The subject of his talk that day was 'The fullness and richness of a human being'. I was happy with the welcome coincidence that this seemed so close to my personal search.

He started with a recitation of a Shloka in Sanskrit, from one of the holy ancient scriptures.

"Om, Purnamadah, purnamidam, purnaat purnamudacyate, Purnasya purnamadaya, purnamevavasisyate. Om shantih, shantih, shantih."

He then translated this.

"That is whole in itself, This is also whole in itself. This whole comes out of That whole. This whole is taken from That whole, what remains is also whole. Peace, peace, peace (every where)."

"Mind boggling – at first. Is it not?" He asked.

He then continued: "'This' refers to Jeevatma – a human being as the individual soul, and 'That' refers to Brahman – the Supreme Divine power, the origin of all souls. The individual soul is complete in itself, whole and perfect, and so is the Supreme Divine, also whole and perfect. 'This' individual soul emerges from 'That' Supreme Power, but none is diminished, and the wholeness remains intact at both levels."

After a brief pause, he added: "The truth therefore, is that each one of you is the divine manifestation of that Supreme Divine Power and each one of you is whole and perfect in yourself as a soul. This soul is your real Self; this is who you are, and this is your real identity."

I was listening with rapt attention.

He continued: "You know that you are not just your body, nor your mind, nor your brain. You are the soul in your body. If you find the word 'soul' too abstract, you may understand it as Chaitanya or Pragya, which mean consciousness or just awareness. Your real identity is defined by your consciousness, and that is the essence of your being."[13]

He then referred to and explained many texts on the subject in the scriptures, and he also clarified the relationship between the human body and the soul.[14]

He then said: "Let me explain this by an illustration, which will make it very clear and easy to understand."

"Look at this Diya – the oil lamp. This has the cup of the lamp, the wick, and the oil in the cup, but it is not lighted. Now let me take it to a lighted Diya with a flame, and let me light the first Diya with the flame burning in the already lighted Diya. So now, you have first Diya also lighted with a flame. You can now see the flame in this Diya is exactly like the flame in the other one."

He was holding up both the Diya in his hands, for us to see clearly.

"Where did the flame in the first Diya come from?" He asked.

Someone in the audience replied: "Swami Ji, it came from the other Diya."

"So, it was taken from the other Diya. But did that diminish that Diya or its flame?" He asked.

The obvious answer was, 'No'.

Swami Ji continued: "So that flame was whole before, and it remains whole after. And what about the flame which emerged in the first Diya? Is it also whole like the one in the other Diya?"

Again, the answer was obvious, 'Yes'.

"So, a whole flame comes out of the other whole flame, and what remains is also a whole." He paused for a moment, and then continued: "That is exactly the position when an individual soul emerges and manifests from the Supreme Divine power. The individual soul is You – the Jeevatma, and the source of that is the Supreme Divine power – the Brahman. Both are complete and whole in themselves, and remain so always. This is the meaning of this Shloka which I read out at the beginning."

There was complete silence. Everyone was trying to absorb the impact of this fascinating visual illustration of one's own self, and its origin from and its connectivity to the Supreme Divine power.

Swami Ji helpfully added: "Your body is like a Diya – the candle or the oil lamp, and the flame is your soul or real self or consciousness – howsoever you understand it. As you exist in this world, your body and soul are together like the Diya and the flame. And, you are that flame."

He paused to let us absorb this fascinating knowledge.

He then continued: "A Diya or candle is lifeless without a flame, and so is your body – dead without the soul. A Diya becomes active when the flame emerges, and similarly, a body comes to life when the soul emerges. The Diya goes back to inactive state when the flame goes away, and a body dies when the soul departs. Both the Diya and the flame are necessary for each other, and both the body and soul together make us a living human being. Your true self is your soul or consciousness, like the flame in the Diya."

The idea was becoming clear, and I could feel myself opening up to a new realization of who I am. I could see my body as the oil lamp and my true self as the flame, both so closely linked together, yet so distinct from each other.

Swami Ji continued: "And just as the flame can be understood as a field of energy which is being radiated in space from a lighted Diya, your consciousness can be understood as an energy field which is emerging from the energy flowing in your body. If you so like, you may call this energy field a human energy field. Just as your eye works in a light field, your entire body functions in this consciousness field. If the light field is absent, the eye will be there but would not work. Similarly, if the consciousness field is gone, the body will be there but lying dead, and will not function. Emergence of consciousness is birth, and regression of consciousness is death."

There was complete silence.

This was truly mind-shattering for me. Suddenly, it became so obvious, so clear, and so simple to understand. This one illustration made it clear to me that my body is like a candle or an oil lamp, and my consciousness is like the flame. I also understood that my body is necessary to support my flame of consciousness. So, my body must be protected, preserved and nourished just like an oil lamp has to be nourished and replenished to keep the flame burning. However, the reality of my Self is not the body, but the flame of consciousness.

Following the words of Swami Ji, I was able to see my own consciousness as an energy field, which emerges when the energy flows within the body. With my knowledge and medical background, it also became obvious to me that this energy field depends upon the level and quality of the energy flow and the structure within which it is flowing. Therefore, the level and quality of my consciousness were closely linked to the level and quality of energy flowing in my body. If the energy flow was down, state of my consciousness would be low. If energy flow improves, my consciousness level goes up.

And this matched well with my own experience of varying levels of my consciousness from one time to another. I could now see how yoga and meditation could help with the energy flow and thereby elevate the consciousness to higher levels of intensity and experiences.

Things were becoming clear to me as if I had seen my own flame, and its light had dispelled the darkness in my mind. I seemed to have discovered myself.

In that moment, I realized that I am that consciousness which makes me alive and which is the essence of my Self.

Concluding his lecture, Swami Ji posed some questions and left everyone to think about the answers.

He asked everyone: "In your meditation next time, you should meditate upon your own true Self, and your consciousness – as an energy field within which your entire being exists and functions. Try to focus on where the flame comes from and where it goes away. Where was the flame before it emerged on the oil lamp, and where did it go away when it left the lamp? And, where was the energy field, which is your true Self, before it emerged in your body at birth, and where would this go away at death? And, what then, is the true meaning of birth and death in this world?"

There was nothing more for anyone to speak.

There was enough to think about and meditate.

I left the lecture hall as a new person, with an awareness I had never felt before.

LISTENING TO SWAMI JI that morning was an overwhelming experience for me. I decided to stay in my room that afternoon. I found that the book given to me by Maa Amrita the previous day, was an exposition of Vedanta philosophy, and was quite a tough reading. As I was turning the pages, a section titled 'Nirvana Satakam' containing six Shlokas or stanzas, caught my attention. Each of these described what I am not, and each of these ended with the same message in the last line:

"Chidananda rupah sivoham, sivoham,"

which meant, "I am the pure limitless consciousness in eternal bliss."

Having heard Swami Ji's lecture, and the picture of the flame still fresh in my mind, I was immediately able to understand these verses. I read this section several times to grasp the full importance of it. Since I cannot describe them better, let me give the English translation of these six stanzas, as follows.

"I am neither the mind, nor the intellect,
nor memory, nor ego.
Nor am I ears, nor tongue.
I am not the nose nor eyes, nor the earth,
space, fire, nor wind.
I am the pure limitless consciousness in eternal bliss."

"I am neither the five pranas (air) nor the life breath.
I am not the seven constituents of body, nor am I the
five sheaths (layers).
I am not the organ of speech nor am I hands and legs.
I am not the genital, nor anus.
I am the pure limitless consciousness in eternal bliss."

"I do not have likes and dislikes, greed and delusion.
I do not have pride. Nor do I have jealousy.
I do not have pursuits of dharma, artha, kama and
moksha (religion, money, desire, and liberation).
I am the pure limitless consciousness in eternal bliss."

"There is no paap or punya (evil or noble deed),
happiness or sorrow, for me.

> *Nor mantra (holy chant), holy place, Vedas or yajnas (fire offering) exist for me. I am neither an experience, nor am I the object, nor the one who is experiencing nor the one who is experienced.*
> *I am the pure limitless consciousness in eternal bliss."*

> *"I have neither death, nor doubt, nor do I have any caste differences in me.*
> *There is no father, mother or birth for me.*
> *There is no student, no teacher, no relative and no friend for me.*
> *I am the pure limitless consciousness in eternal bliss."*

> *"I am free of thoughts and free of forms.*
> *I am connected to all sense organs as I pervade everywhere.*
> *I am not connected to bondage or freedom.*
> *I am the pure limitless consciousness in eternal bliss."*

The commentary for these stanzas explained in detail that all the above noted features are physical attributes which exist at the level of human body and mind, and all these are experienced at that level. All these are therefore, relevant and necessary in so far as the human body has to function in the world. But the real self is the consciousness, which is pure and unblemished by any of these attributes. This pure consciousness is the real identity of self and is experienced as eternal bliss. What is needed is to look beyond the human body and its attributes and to become aware of one's true self. That is the way to discover and attain the state of bliss and harmony within one's own self.

There was another stanza which literally repeated what Swami ji had said about the oil lamp and the flame. This was part of a prayer offered to such a lamp, and the first line of that prayer read as follows:

"Deepajyotih parambrahma, deepajyotir janardanah,"

This means as follows:

"This flame of the lamp is like That self-evident Brahman – the Supreme Divine Power. Its light manifests everything."

It was becoming quite clear to me that the scriptures in the spiritual field saw 'light' as the essential manifestation of the divine power both at the individual and at cosmic levels. I decided to explore this further with Dr. Sonali. My opportunity arose the same evening. After we had our dinner, she invited me to stay on to talk.

I told her about Swami Ji's lecture that morning, and she was happy to know that I understood it so well and found it so interesting.

I also told her: "Sonali, the more I hear about my energy field and my consciousness as defining my real self, the more I feel convinced about that. The scriptures keep referring to 'light' as the manifestation of divine power. But, I am not very clear how light is understood in the world of science, and how it compares with the understanding of light in the spiritual world. Is there a meeting point between these two view points?"

She replied: "Yes, I understand what you want to know. I have been working on this for quite some time. Light is something we all know and experience in our daily life. If we use light as the medium of expression, it can be very helpful in understanding this subject from a scientific point of view, as well as from a spiritual perspective."

"Let me first mention the scientific understanding of light." She continued: "Science has found that light is an electro-magnetic radiation in space. Light particles are known as photons that move at the speed of light, which is known to be 186,000 miles per second. Einstein found that nothing can move faster than this, and so regarded the speed of light as the limiting factor for all movements of energy and matter. He also studied the interaction of light with matter – the photo electric process – and relied upon it for explaining various processes at work in nature."[15]

She saw me listening with rapt attention, and continued: "Quantum physics later found that a photon can move as a particle and also as a wave. Light therefore, was seen as a wave in motion, and its movement could be described in terms of its frequency and the corresponding wavelength. The frequency of a wave is measured in terms of 'cycles,' which means the number of times the wave is oscillating or vibrating in a second. It also was discovered that there was a very large spectrum of such frequency in which these waves traveled in space."[16]

In order to understand its relevance, I asked: "How does this spectrum of light waves relate to my energy field, or so to say, my field of consciousness?"

Trying to be as concise as possible, she replied: "The basic fact remains that all these light waves from the lowest to the highest frequency range are transmitted through oscillations in the electro-magnetic field which is an energy field. Therefore, if you accept your own energy field as the ground of your consciousness, you also realize that all these transmissions are happening within the field of your consciousness."

"What are these transmissions that you are talking about?" I asked.

She explained: "All your thoughts and actions are transmissions happening within your field of consciousness. Nothing is beyond that field. In other words, none of your thoughts or actions can exist outside your consciousness field. As such, these thoughts and actions are similar to waves existing and moving within an energy field."

She looked at me intently and added: "Aparna, this has very far reaching implications in the spiritual context. This would mean that everything exists within the field of consciousness; and just like the universal light field, the Supreme Consciousness defines the limits of all movements of everything at the cosmic level."

I was quite impressed with her study and knowledge of the subject, and asked her to continue.

She continued: "I need not point out to you the importance of light in the scientific context. As you very well know, uses and applications of light waves have been highly developed in many fields of science and technology. For instance, light waves are now successfully used not only for emission of light, but also for transmitting information through fiber optics. Another far reaching development of laser, which is the acronym for 'light amplitude synchronized emission of radiation,' has led to most valuable applications of laser beams technology in many industrial and medical areas."[17]

She thought that this was probably becoming too technical for me.

So she summed up: "The basic fact is that light in all its forms represents vibrations that are moving in space, and this is what is commonly referred to as a light field. Like an energy field, this can be scientifically identified and measured in terms of field equations, which describe the field in mathematical terms. This holds good for light in all its forms, such as light flowing down from sun, or moon, or stars, light appearing in nature around us, or light emanating from numerous devices and systems invented by science and technology. Light thus occupies a central position in the scientific knowledge and understanding of the world in which we live."

I was finding it quite interesting and I wanted to know more.

So, I said: "Sonali, this means that all around us, there are numerous fields of light, originating from various sources. Can you tell me if these fields connect with each other? Or, how do these interact between themselves?"

She thought for a moment, and then replied: "Yes. This is very interesting. These fields exist and are defined in terms of a field equation for each field. However, these fields also interconnect and make up a larger collective field. So, a field has its own identity, but at the same time, it is also a part of the larger collective field. The field equations for each field can be added up by a mathematical process of vector addition, and that will give you the field equation for the combined collective field."[18]

"Can you help me understand this with an example?" I asked.

She promptly responded: "Yes. Take the same example which you have seen in Swami Ji's lecture. Each flame has its own light field, but the light fields of all the flames interconnect in space, and make a combined collective light field as well. Therefore, each flame has its own identity, and simultaneously, it is present in the combined light field of all flames."

I had studied light as part of my education in elementary physics, but this was an entirely new perspective for me to see light as an energy field. Until then, I had also not realized the fact that all light fields interconnect and make up a larger combined light field. It was virtually as if Sonali had thrown a new light on my knowledge of light!

She paused and stood up to bring drinking water for us. She asked me if I was tired, but I insisted for her to continue.

She then proceeded to explain how the scriptures in the spiritual field considered light as the most obvious manifestation of the Supreme Divine Power.

She said: "You may be surprised to find how much the scriptures keep referring to light to explain the divine power both at the individual level of a soul as well as the cosmic level of Brahman. The basic idea is quite simple. The Supreme Divine Power is described as Brahman, and manifests itself as extremely subtle vibrations of energy which show up as light everywhere. That is why it is regarded as omnipresent. In its purest state, it can be understood simply as vibrating energy without form, until it manifests in the material world of nature. When it manifests and flows at the level of an individual human being, our scriptures refer to it as Soul. This is the source of all life and the reality of all manifestations including the human form and body."

She showed me a few references to 'light' appearing in some ancient holy scriptures. One of them caught my attention as it seemed easy to understand. It read as follows:

> *"Na tatra suryo bhati, na Chandra tarakam.*
> *Nema vidyuto bhati kutoyamagnih,*
> *tameva bhantam anubhati sarvam, ….*
> *tasya bhasa sarvamidam vibhati."*[19]

The English translation reads as follows.

> *"The sun does not shine there; nor these stars, nor moon.*
> *The light does not shine there; what to talk of the fire?*
> *That shining, everything else shines from it ...*
> *By the light of That – all This is that shines everywhere."*

This beautiful expression had a strong impact on me and I kept repeating it in my mind.

> *"By the light of That – all This is that shines everywhere."*

Once again, I saw in my mind the vivid picture of flame of the oil lamp, and a succession of many flames on many oil lamps, each one having been lighted by the other, and all of them originating from the same source. I realized, this was the 'light' scriptures were referring to.

My mind, working as a medical doctor, went back in a flash to my experience of handling a child birth. I had handled so many of them in my practice, and I had many a times shared the great joy and happiness of seeing a newly born baby as the nature's most precious gift of life to human beings. I had often wondered where the life really came from; and even though I knew almost everything about the process from conception to delivery of a child, but I had never really found the answer. Now, suddenly, I could see in my mind, the 'mother flame' lighting up the 'child flame', just like the lighting of a lamp. It dawned upon me that just as a lamp is lighted with the flame when the necessary structure and properties of the lamp are present, in exactly the same way, life is infused as an active energy field in the embryo when the necessary body structure has been made ready by the nature. The 'mother flame' then lights the 'child flame.'

I was pleased with this new vision – what a wonderful way to look at the process of life continuing from times immemorial – each flame lighting a new one. I thought, if all the flames glowed and radiated their light all around, as they should, the darkness in our lives would go away. Hopefully, I wished, we can see the light, and make that happen.

Sonali looked at me lost in my thoughts.

It was my turn to speak and I thanked her for such a clear and interesting exposition of a rather difficult subject.

I said: "Sonali, you have really made me see my own energy field, and I have now also understood the meaning and significance of light which I see all around and often also experience within my own heart. If this is the true meaning of my soul, and if this is the ground for my consciousness and my true self that I have been searching for, you have made it possible for me to make a lot of progress in that direction."

I added in a lighter vein: "Now I also see why light is such a central theme in our everyday life. We always talk about removing darkness and moving into light. Also in our religious and spiritual ceremonies and even in our festivals, we worship light. We seek light everywhere, and now I know that our own reality is in fact defined by our energy field, and that shows up as a light field. Perhaps, now I can say – I know who I am."

She kept looking at me with obvious appreciation.

After a pause, I added: "I can also see how our individual light fields interconnect – just like two or more energy fields interconnect and add up to make a collective field in the world of science. It now seems clear to me that your light field and my light field have interconnected, and these now make up a light field of our collective consciousness, which we now share. I can very well believe now that not only you and I, but all of us are interconnected at the level of our light fields; and that connection is at the most fundamental level of our existence – our consciousness. And, not only are we so connected with each other, but we are also connected simultaneously with, and are part of the collective light field of all light fields – which we can very well call the universal field of cosmic consciousness."

I was quite thrilled at this discovery, and told her: "Sonali, today, you have shown me that my true self is my energy field within which my mind and body exist and function. I also understand how this energy field emerges at birth and regresses at death, and sustains me all through my life."

I added: "This realization has answered for me three most important questions of my life:

First: I know who I am. Once I know myself as an energy field, it takes out all the mystery about the notion of my soul or some other abstract heavenly power inside me.

Second: I now know that just like me, everyone else has his or her own energy field; and all my inter-personal interactions with others are field interactions. My field interacts with their field. This is quite the same as fields interact in the world of science – they connect, communicate, and exchange information as well as energy from each other. This gives me the key to my harmonious relationships and interactions with others in the world. I now know that I must focus upon aligning my energy levels and positive vibrations if I wish to connect with others with harmony and coherence. I am sure that I can do that once I realize the need to do that.

Third: Above all, I now understand that all fields superposition and combine into a supreme universal field. We may call this the Supreme Divine Power, or by any other name. But I am now convinced that I am always connected with it as an integral part of it. This not only gives me instant connectivity with the Divine but a great feeling of liberation."

She hugged me with great affection, and said: "It has been such a good experience discussing this with you. You are so intelligent, and talking to you has in fact helped me clear my own thoughts as well."

I felt very light as I left her room. I had a beautiful feeling, I had found my self.

That night, in the middle of the darkness of night, I slept with light inside me.

THE NEXT MORNING, at 5am I went to the yoga and meditation center in the garden behind the Ashram. As I walked along the garden path, everything around seemed to be completely peaceful. The soft morning breeze was spreading all over the fragrance from beautiful flowers in the garden, which still seemed to be resting under the drops of dew so lovingly showered on them by the night. It was a heavenly feeling for me to be there before sunrise. In a quiet corner of the garden, I settled down to do my meditation.

I sat down on a mattress on the floor, cross-legged, with my hands and fingers in yogic posture, with my back straight and eyes lightly closed. I had learnt meditation earlier, but could feel that this day it was going to be a very different experience than ever before.

I gradually became aware of my presence in Rishikesh, then in the Ashram, then in the garden, and then my surroundings. I then shifted my awareness to the things around me, the grass, the plants and the flowers all around, and visualized the soft dew gently sitting on the flowers. I felt the cool morning breeze as it touched my body. I then became aware of my body, and then my own breath, and watched it silently. I focused on my breath, and became aware of each breath as I breathed in, and breathed out. Gradually, I started feeling like a silent witness to my own breath as it was coming in and as it was going out, smoothly, on its own, and without any effort or thought on my part. I then became totally aware of the rhythm of my breath coming in and coming out.

By now, a feeling of relaxed calmness had taken over me and I was totally absorbed in my awareness at that moment. Soon, I became aware of the energy making my breath move in and out, and how this energy was flowing inside me. I felt the energy flowing through each part of my body, starting from the feet, moving upwards gradually, and going all the way up to the top of my head. I became aware of the smooth yet powerful energy flow through my body, and I felt so very alive and alert to this energy flow.

Then I became aware of the Chakras – the energy centers – seen as the focal points of energy flow in my body; one by one, starting from the root chakra at the base of my spine, and then moving up to the emotion chakra below the navel, then the fire chakra at the navel, the next higher air chakra at the heart region, the sound chakra at the throat region, the light chakra between the eye brows, and finally the crown chakra at the top of my head. I focused for a few moments on each one of these, before moving to the next one, and I could feel each of them flashing and sending out energy all over.

By this time, I had identified myself so completely with these energy flows, that I virtually had no feeling of my physical body. I felt, as if my body had dissolved, and I was just an energy flow, floating free. It is then, that I experienced a new sensation – a feeling of energy radiating outward from my body – like light flowing out from my body into the space around it. I let this feeling linger on, and just continued being aware of it.

Slowly, this appeared as a light field around my entire body, which I could actually feel as a bright aura around me. I felt that I was seeing my own human energy field. I had very little sensation of my body presence, and it was as if everything had been transformed into an energy field, a vibrating and shining field of light, all around me, within which I felt very comfortable and secure. I felt I could stay in that for ever.

As my awareness became deeper and completely focused on this all-embracing field of energy around me, I felt it expanding, as if its boundaries were moving outwards and were gradually dissolving into a larger energy field spread all around, as far as I could see. I literally transcended my own energy field and moved into some kind of a cosmic or universal field of energy. I felt as if all the energy fields in the universe had merged together into a field which was universal, without any boundaries, or beginning or end. In that moment, I had a most comfortable feeling of being connected and becoming an integral part of this universal cosmic energy field.

I had reached a state of perfect peace and calm, and I had a feeling of total freedom from any burden or bondage. I was free, and floating, and I felt full and complete in my self. This was me, and this was my true self, a field of pure consciousness within which my body, mind, and everything else existed. It was so clear. My true self transcended my body, my mind, and my intellect, and it was not limited by any of these. It was an energy field, which was inseparably connected with the cosmic and universal energy field, ever before and ever after. In that moment, I had become aware of my real self, as an energy field, which constantly emerged from and submerged into that cosmic and universal energy field, now and always, without any beginning or end.

With this experience in my meditation, the *Mahavakyas* – the great truths enunciated in ancient scriptures – became visible to me with utmost clarity:

One, *"Aham Brahmasmi"* meaning, *"I am one with the Supreme Divine Power"* and Two, *"Tat Twam Asi"*, literally meaning, *"Thou are That"* and implying, *"You are that Ultimate Divine."*

This was as close to being liberated as one could conceive.

And above all, I had found myself.

CHAPTER 2

Why the Conflict?

AFTER SPENDING THREE DAYS in the Ashram, I returned to Delhi and was totally engrossed in the hospital work. Whenever I could get free time, my thoughts kept going back to the lovely time I had spent at the Ashram. I also kept thinking about the many new realizations about myself that I had experienced through my interactions there. All this gave me a different state of mind, and I carried a distinct feeling of lightness even in the midst of my busy routine at the hospital.

While I could feel that I was getting better within myself, things in the world around me seemed to be deteriorating and getting worse. The TV and newspapers were full of reports of serious unrest and turmoil happening in many countries. There were conflicts arising everywhere. In Egypt, there was a massive uprising against the President who had ruled the country for over 30 years. Soon thereafter, similar conflict happened in neighboring countries like Libya, Jordan and Bahrain. The situation everywhere was explosive and showed serious confrontation between the people and the established regimes. The resulting violence was causing deaths of thousands of people, including woman and children. Army had to step in, and the situation looked like a civil war.

War was in fact going on in some other parts of the world, like Afghanistan, where people were still trying to find a solution to the causes of conflict. Many other places like North and South Korea seemed to be at the brink of violent confrontation.

Terrorism had raised its ugly head and shocked the entire world with the 9/11 strike on the Twin Towers of the World Trade Center in New York City that killed thousands of innocent people. Terrorist attacks had spread out to other countries, including England and India. Underground train blasts in London, and killings in Mumbai with terrorist attacks on Taj and Oberoi Hotels and other places in the city, caused loss of life of hundreds of people. The madness was continuing unabated and the confrontations were getting worse. These were no longer confined to hijacking for extortion of money or other purposes, but had now degenerated into a mindless and crazy madness to kill innocent people and destroy human life for no rhyme or reason.

While human beings were busy killing each other, natural disasters were occurring with a fury never seen before. The ecological balance had been severely disturbed by reckless exploitation of nature by man, and the consequences were showing up as global warming and rising levels of pollution. A hard-hitting message was given by nature when Japan was struck with an earthquake of exceptionally great intensity that was followed by a tsunami wave and devastation in a nuclear power plant. All this had resulted in spread of highly dangerous radiation, loss of thousands of lives, billions of dollars worth of damage, and unimaginable misery and suffering for millions of people.

As if the political and military turmoil and natural disasters were not enough, the social fabric was being torn apart by wide spread corruption and reckless exploitation. Money power and political power seemed to have joined together in a sinister conspiracy to amass wealth by resorting to corruption at all levels.

In our own country, we were getting repeated shocks from the discovery of rampant corruption in money matters relating to some very high profile transactions at the national level. There was a shocking discovery of huge corruption in the holding of Commonwealth Games, involving over 15 billion dollars siphoned away. Before we could recover from that shock, we came to know about the massive corruption in the allocation of 2G spectrum for cellular mobile phone services, for which the loss to the country was estimated at over 35 billion dollars. Equally disturbing was the discovery of a number of scams relating to many land and property deals, including the making of a multistory housing tower for war widows and veterans. Even more scandalous was the discovery that millions of dollars of ill-gotten black money was being shifted and stashed away in some tax haven countries.

I was very uncomfortable and agitated about these situations but did not know what to do. I realized that the more we knew about these incidents the more we got depressed and frustrated. We felt helpless and let down. All through our education and training, we were brought up with a belief in our systems—social, economic and political, and the protection by rule of law. We had built up our lives on the faith that these systems worked well and provided us the framework for our existence and growth. We were taught to respect and abide by these systems as responsible citizens and good human beings. Now we were discovering that all these systems were not working. We felt devastated and cheated to find that these systems had actually not worked for us, but allowed the worst kind of people to control enormous money and political power and misuse that to exploit us.

This situation was revealing a fundamental conflict in the

actual working of the systems that vitally affected each one of us. This could not be ignored or left to be taken care of by someone else. We needed to understand the causes, and deal with them. If we did nothing to correct the situation, this would result in throwing away our values to the winds, and facing a serious challenge to our faith in the systems in which we live and work in our daily life. I had a distinct feeling that things were undergoing a radical change, and such change was happening for the worse – not for better.

It was not long before I faced a glaring example of such change which directly affected me and my work.

The hospital where I have been working is known as Angels Hospital. It is highly respected for its quality and standard of medical facilities and services. It has seven departments and each is under the charge of a well-qualified and experienced doctor.

These departments are: cardiology, neurology, gynecology and maternity welfare, orthopedics, ENT i.e. eyes, nose and throat, dental care, and pathology. The hospital was set up about 20 years ago by a Parsi gentleman, Mr. Jehangir Sonawala, who was a successful business man and great philanthropist. He ensured that the hospital had world-class equipment and best procedures in all the departments. In order to make the facilities available to all sections of society, he provided that 20 percent of the hospital beds were kept for free and charitable work for those who could not afford to pay the hospital fee and charges.

Mr. Sonawala died about six years ago. The ownership and control of the hospital then passed on to his two sons. They followed their father's approach and we continued doing quite well all these years. Due to some internal family reasons, the sons recently decided to relinquish the hospital ownership.

Majority ownership and control of the hospital were then acquired by an American company, Harpis Hospitals. This American company had been running hospitals in several other countries and had decided to enter India with the acquisition of ownership and control in our hospital.

Mr. Peter Collins, Vice-president of Harpis Hospitals, had recently taken over as the Managing Director of our hospital. We had briefly met him at a reception hosted for him when the deal was closed a month ago. We later came to know that he had made a new business plan for the working of our hospital. A special meeting was called to discuss the new plan, and all the seven department heads were asked to attend this meeting, along with the members of the Board and senior executives. As I was the head of the department of gynecology and maternity welfare, I was also present at this meeting in the hospital's main conference room.

Mr. Peter Collins started the proceedings.

He said: "Ladies and Gentlemen, I welcome you all to this meeting and I thank you for coming here this morning. I know, each one of you is quite busy and therefore, we will keep this meeting as short as possible."

He continued: "I will come straight to an important matter for which we need help and support from all of you. This is for our new business plan which I propose to put in effect from the beginning of next month."

The plan was displayed on the screen in the conference room.

He then continued: "This has two parts. Part One shows our expansion plan. As you can see, we plan to set up three more hospitals in this country in three metropolitan towns, within the next two years. This requires a total investment of about $100 million US dollars. I am happy to inform you that we have informally cleared this with our bankers and the means of finance have been broadly tied up. We have engaged our international consultants to work out the best configuration of facilities and procedures, and on that basis, to work out the details of equipment required. Once we have identified the sites in each of these towns, the architects will step in to start working on the layout drawings. We will share these with you at the appropriate time as we make progress."

He then moved on to Part Two of the Plan.

He continued: "Part Two shows our projected revenues for the next one year. This is where you come in. We plan to double the revenues starting next month. Our review in the last two weeks has shown that this hospital is providing excellent treatments and services, but the fees and charges are very low. We are going to increase these by 50 to 150 percent. A detailed schedule of fees for each department and for each procedure has been prepared and you will find it in the separate compilation being given to you. You have to follow this new schedule of fees from now onwards. Please feel free to give me your feedback, and to ask for any help you may need to implement these in your department."

We looked at the new schedule of fees to be charged from the patients. This was almost double, and in some cases two-and-half times the present fee level. We were shocked. What was happening, and why?

I looked at Dr. Banerjee, the senior-most doctor in our hospital and head of the department of neurology.

He took the initiative, and spoke out: "Mr. Collins, we are happy to see your plans for setting up three more hospitals, and we assure you our full support on that. But we can not double the fees and charges for the patients. Can you tell us how the new proposed fee and charges have been worked out?"

Mr. Collins said: "There is no mystery. These are about the same rates that we charge for similar treatments and procedures in our hospitals in America. These are converted and shown in equivalent Indian currency. And why shouldn't we do so? Your hospital is providing the facilities and services of world-class standard; and for this, the credit goes to all of you. Patients must then also pay the fee based on the same world-wide standard. You know, nothing can come for free."

And then he added: "Yes, let me tell you another thing. I find that your hospital is giving 20 percent of the beds and treatments free. This is going to be stopped. Every one has to pay now. We are not here for charity, and I hope you understand."

This was like a bombshell dropped on us.

Dr. Banerjee was visibly agitated. Somehow, he kept his cool.

He said: "This is a different country, Mr. Collins. And, our hospital has always looked after the interests of the weaker section of our society. This is the vision with which the hospital was created 20 years ago, and this is the ethos we have been following."

Dr. Mehta was the head of the department of cardiology, and commanded great respect.

He intervened: "We are not against growth. But, Mr. Collins, we are running a hospital –and we believe in doing a service to all those who need it. Your plan will make it impossible for a very large number of people to use our hospital. The proposed fees and charges are so high that only the rich and affluent will be able to afford them. And, if you shut out the 20 percent free facility, this place will cater only to the elite, not to the wider cross section of society that we serve. Please give it careful thought before you implement the new plan."

Mr. Collins retorted: "I have already thought about all this. If I combine the facilities for patients who pay the full fee with those that are free on charity, the whole facility will lose its class. You should know very well that a hotel can not have one wing for five-star facilities and another wing for a three-star facility. These belong to separate classes, and do not mix."

Then he added in a firm voice: "My dear friends, let me remind you that in order to grow, you first need to make profit. The more profit you make, the faster you can grow. I am not asking you to give up your service motive and effort. Please continue doing that as best as you can. But my job is to run the business, and business means making money. So please, let me do my job, and you do yours."

There was complete silence.

When no one spoke, Mr. Collins continued: "I don't see any problem. We can work together so long as we understand that you look after the interests of the patients, and I look after the interests of the owners."

This was indeed a shock for us all. The way he put it, I could immediately sense a serious conflict between the interests of the patients and the interests of the owners who were out to make money for themselves and cared nothing about service to patients. I was feeling quite depressed to think that we were now going to run this hospital along the concept of a hotel.

Someone among us must have mumbled that we were not running a hotel.

Mr. Collins overheard that, and said: "Hotel or hospital… For me, both are business. No difference."

We again looked at Dr. Banerjee, our senior-most colleague. He understood our feelings, and said: "But Sir, in order to run the hospital whichever way you want, we need to keep our doors open for patients to come in. I am afraid, with your very high and expensive fee scales, patients will not be able to afford our services, and we will lose them to other hospitals. Even your business angle would not work then. Again, I say India is a different country – it's not America."

Mr. Collins looked at him with a smile, and said: "Good that you now mention my business angle. I have figured out all that. We have a separate company in the Harpis group that offers medical insurance policies. This has worked well in other countries, and we are immediately starting this here. People can take insurance, and then it is the insurance company, which pays the hospital. Patients no longer need to worry about high fees and charges."

He did not elaborate that those high fees and charges are then passed on to the people as part of the high premiums payable for the insurance policy. But there was no point in raising that before him. It was clear that he was bringing both a hospital company and a medical insurance company, and both of these were going to operate hand-in-glove. The clear mandate for both was to make as much money as possible.

Mr. Collins closed the meeting with a word of formal thanks.

All of us left without saying a word, but feeling quite disturbed in our minds.

Later that evening, when I narrated this to Raj, he was also quite unhappy.

He said: "Aparna, this is very unfortunate. This means that your medical profession is now being totally hijacked and taken over by big business. If persons like you wish to focus on interests of patients, you will have to face a clear conflict of interest between your patients and the business owners."

After a pause, he added: "But actually, I am not surprised. This is not only happening in your medical profession, same thing is happening in other professions as well. Take for example, the accounting profession. It is now dominated and practically taken over by big multinational accounting firms. They operate in a large number of countries, have offices all over, and employ thousands of professional and other staff all over the world. They exercise huge power and between themselves are able to practically monopolize all the professional work for multinational corporations and big businesses. Their practice is also driven for making money, and the service element comes in only next, if at all."

Then he continued: "A similar thing is happening in the field of education. Big business is entering this field and turning it into a money-making business. I can see that this is now also going to happen in my legal profession. All of this is being defended in the name of globalization of business, industry and services. I do not know what I can do to deal with this."

Hearing him, I felt quite depressed.

I said: "Raj, I am not against globalization and growth. That should result in benefit for everyone, as that would enable us to get the best knowledge and skill across national boundaries. The problem is not globalization or growth, but the conflicts that these can create if driven by greed and lust for money."

Raj said: "I see your point. But this is a very difficult issue. We need to think more about it."

He then opened his laptop and got busy attending to his email.

I WANTED TO CONTINUE my exploration of our current situation, but was not able to see when that would be possible. I needed to spend more time with Raj, to discuss things in detail to find out the causes, and explore possible ways to handle the situation. We also needed to carefully consider their impact on our own lives.

That opportunity came up sooner than I expected. After three weeks, we were going to celebrate our 15th wedding anniversary. Much to my delight, Raj suggested that we take a holiday and spend time together on this occasion. Both of us wanted to go away to a quiet place in the mountains, and we decided to go to Anandipur, a small hill-station in the Kumaon hills. We realized that we both were so busy with work that unless we went away to such a place, we would not get much time together. Ever since our marriage 15 years ago, responsibilities of our work, family and other commitments always took priority over our personal life. This trip was going to give us the much-needed time with each other that we always wanted.

As I found myself settling down comfortably in the natural bliss of beautiful Himalayan Mountains in Anandipur, and enjoying the company of my husband, I almost wished I never had to go back home again. This picturesque town, far away from urban civilization, seemed to provide everything that I could have possibly wanted at that stage of my life. And, I began to think: "Could it be that the simplest things in life can make us so happy? Does it really take so little to feel so peaceful?"

When I shared my thoughts with Raj, I realized that we both had similar thoughts. How good it felt to have a partner with whom one could agree upon something! During this time, we discussed many things. I also took the opportunity to explain to him that I had many unanswered questions about our life and existence, which I needed to explore further. Some of these were indeed very basic questions that each individual asks at least once in one's lifetime. I wondered, whether the answers to some of the most basic questions in life could also be so simple that we fail to recognize them because of their sheer simplicity?

That evening, after a light dinner, we were sitting in the balcony outside our room. The air was crisp and cool, and the distant lights of houses on the mountain range seemed so soothing. There was stillness in the atmosphere, and misty fragrance of pine trees was floating in the air. Both of us were quietly enjoying the peaceful surroundings.

Then Raj looked at me and asked: "What are you thinking?"

I said: "I am really happy we have come here. We have so much to talk about, and we will have the time to do that here. The visit to the Ashram has done me a lot of good. I am thinking, what I need to do now to take things forward."

"Tell me, what do you want to do?" He asked me.

"Let me say, I can now feel and understand my real self – maybe, as an energy field of consciousness, or something like that beyond my body and mind. So, perhaps I know who I am. But I am quite confused about the world in which I am living. What is that? Why does it seem to be such a struggle, all the time? Why do I have to keep searching for harmony and happiness in my life? And whenever I seem to have found them, they just slip away. And that seems to be the position not only with me, but with many others whom I know or work with."

After a pause, I added in a depressed tone: "I cannot accept what is happening in my hospital. The new owners are bent upon converting it into a money-making business. It will badly hurt the patients and create conflict for all of us."

He touched my hand, as if trying to calm me down.

My voice reflected a painful disappointment, as I said: "Raj, why is it that we always seem to be chasing things or sorting out our problems with others? That never seems to end. There is always something new to worry about. All this keeps causing so much tension and stress, and sometimes I feel quite tired and frustrated with my own situation in life. Why should it be that way?"

Raj understood this quite well.

He replied: "You know, in my work as a lawyer, I see this all the time. Everybody seems to be fighting with everyone else, and a major part of our energies are spent in dealing with these disputes, whether in a court of law, or in arbitration, or in any other dispute resolution process. You would be shocked to know that some of the most brilliant minds are busy in this area of legal practice, and huge amounts of money and time are spent on these disputes. There is so much conflict everywhere, and that seems to have become a part of our lives."

"Is there some way to get out of this?" I asked with a sense of discomfort: "I do not think, our lives are meant to be wasted away in never-ending conflicts in our day-to-day living. Don't you think we need to find out what has gone wrong?"

"Yes, we should. Let us think. But it is time for me to sleep now," he said, and got up to go to bed.

And, then he called out from the bed, just to tease me: "Why are you so worried? You also fight with me so many times, and you should know why you do that – even when I have done nothing wrong."

I smiled back, and said: "Ok. Ok. You are never at fault. I am the one who is wrong, always! Does that make you happy? I don't want to argue with a lawyer now. We will talk it out tomorrow. Now you go to sleep. Good night."

As I got into bed and was trying to sleep, my childhood memories suddenly flashed through my mind.

One of the earliest and pleasant memories that I have of my childhood is that of a great big courtyard in my ancestral home. It was a large square of cobbled bricks surrounded on three sides by many rooms. On one side, there was a vast garden, and beyond it, flowed the river Ganges – the same holy river which flowed through Rishikesh and continued down almost 300 miles to this city. It was our home where we all felt fully secure and happy, and took it for granted that all this came to us naturally. We never thought that life outside our home could be any different for others.

My grandmother was a deceptively frail-looking woman, whose determination and sense of purpose belied her appearance. She would sit cross-legged on a wooden bed at one end of the courtyard, like a queen on her throne, and carry out the mammoth task of running the household. Servants would scurry from one end of house to the other doing their chores, while instructions and admonitions would be shouted out by my grandmother.

If ever I could find time between my daily deeds of mischief, to watch her, I would wonder how she could be so full of purpose in all her activities. Even if it was preparing a special dish for dinner that she was supervising, her expression was that of a warrior preparing for battle. As I look back at those happy times, I simply wonder at the dedication and devotion she brought to bear on whatever she did, and the sense of harmony and happiness that flowed in those simple surroundings and our carefree lives. I now feel nostalgia and a sense of pain, when I realize that we seem to have lost all of that somewhere in our pursuit for success and in our never-ending chase for what we seek in the name of prosperity.

Many years later, when I began to ask myself questions about my existence and purpose, the picture of my grandmother would appear before me, giving instructions and carrying on her business with complete faith, compassion and confidence. In today's world, where confusion grips us at every step, where faith is often questioned, and values are sometimes vague, I search for that sense of purpose and clarity.

I do not know when I fell fast asleep that night.

THE NEXT MORNING, we had a leisurely breakfast in the small dining room of our hotel. As we were about to leave the dining room, another couple walked in. We were simply delighted to find most unexpectedly that Rahul and his wife Neera were there. Rahul was a very close college friend of Raj. While Raj later became a lawyer, Rahul went to America, did his Ph.D. in Economics, and was now teaching at a management institute in Bangalore. Rahul and Neera met at this institute and got married. Rahul told us that he had come to deliver a series of lectures at the Academy for Advanced Studies in Simla, which was nearby, and decided to take the weekend off at Anandipur. It was a sheer coincidence that we met them here, after a gap of almost a year since we last saw them.

Raj and I went out for a long walk in the lovely woods, and later met them for lunch. The afternoon sun was very inviting, and after lunch, all of us settled on the terrace outside the dining hall. The terrace overlooked the valley, and provided a panoramic view of the mountain range beyond. The hotel staff was very helpful and served us some dessert and very good coffee there.

Raj and Rahul were catching up with their stories and Neera updated me on what was happening with them in Bangalore. Surprisingly, I found that both Rahul and Neera were quite critical of the current economic policies and systems and blamed them for the strife and unrest among the workers in the industry as well as the farmers in the fields. At first, we thought that their attitude was due to the influence of Marxist philosophy and revolutionary tendencies, which many economists pick up when they are exposed to

Marxist literature. But we found that Rahul had analyzed the issues much deeper and was greatly dissatisfied with the inadequacies and contradictions in our economic, social and political systems. This led to some very interesting and long discussions, and I was reminded of what Raj had said to me the previous evening about 'conflict' having become a part of our lives.

Raj repeated what he had earlier told me about conflicts and disputes and the judicial process dealing with these.

He then added: "Our lives seem to be a constant ongoing battle. There are never-ending conflicts in our lives and in the world around us. We seek harmony, but we find conflict everywhere, despite all our progress through the ages. That is how the world is, and I have no choice but to reconcile and cope with it as best I can."

Rahul responded: "Yes, you are right. As I see it, the most acute conflict is showing up in the economic field, between all the players in the economic process. Look at the tussle between capital and labor, owners and managers, producers and consumers, government and taxpayers – everyone seems to be facing a conflict of interest. Capital seeks maximization of profit or net worth, but labor must focus on maximizing the wages, and that directly cuts into the primary objective of capital. Owners and managers have conflicting time horizons and irreconcilable differences regarding strategies, accountability and risk exposures. Pricing and quality issues place producers and consumers on opposite sides, and the continuing battle between the government and taxpayers shows no prospect of abating. It appears that everyone is engaged in a zero-sum game – where one person's gain is necessarily another's loss."

As he paused, I asked him: "Rahul, you are such a great economist. Don't you have any solution to all this in your economics? Why does the system not work?"

He replied: "Yes, we have a problem there. I do not want to bore you with a lecture on economic theory. Let me just say that our system is based upon the neo-classical economic theory of profit-maximization, and that is not working properly now. Adam Smith, one of the greatest economists of the last century, had shown that when every player in the economic process worked to maximize his profit, the entire economy moved to a point of equilibrium which achieved the optimum levels of prices and production throughout the economy, and this benefited everyone – both at the micro and macro levels."

I wondered if it worked earlier, why would it not work now?

Rahul seemed to have anticipated my question, and continued: "This does not work now, because the theory was based upon certain assumptions, which are no longer valid. In order for this theory to work, we need a free market, where competition is perfect and consumers and producers have free choices. As you very well know, we do not have these. Today, we have a regulated market and virtual monopolies in a wide range of products and services, both in the private and public sectors. The neo-classical model breaks down in such a situation."

After a brief pause, he continued: "That is not the only problem. Another major issue is that our economic system recognizes only those things which are quantified in money terms. Anything that is not measured in money terms is left out. The result is that our profit maximization concept in this system ignores and leaves out many things even though these are very important for us. For example, the system fails to recognize and account for costs and benefits relating to ecology, environment, pollution, social welfare, education, and healthcare. It is obvious that all of these are very important for our overall growth and quality of life. But our economic system just ignores them. It focuses only on money matters."

"Why can't we correct this? If we know these shortcomings, our economists should be able to work out a solution." I intervened.

Rahul responded: "Yes, we can, but only if we all agree and work together. Unfortunately, no one is willing to face the challenge and pick up the costs. Now that the entire world is opening up as a global market, everyone is busy in a sort of economic warfare between the nations. The interests of the developed and under-developed or third-world developing countries also clash; and these conflicts now show up on a global level in the form of trade barriers, protectionist tariffs and economic blocs formed by vested interests."

We did not know what to say, and kept listening.

He continued: "In fact, in today's world, military warfare is being replaced by economic warfare. This is happening in many ways. For example, middle-east countries have grouped together and have pushed up oil prices for the rest of the world. Powerful global forces are causing massive volatility of stock markets, erosion of market capitalization, unstable currencies, and cracking banking and monetary systems in many countries. There is no use trying to blame one country or the other, but we have to face the fact that this is the situation."

Neera wanted to say something, and we looked at her.

She said: "We are not trying to blame anyone. I think we all are ourselves responsible for all this happening. In fact, we are not only in conflict with each other, but our conflicts extend all the way to our interaction with nature."

I intervened: "What do you mean? What is our conflict with nature around us?"

She was excited, and spoke rather forcefully: "Yes. We are in constant confrontation with nature. We are always trying to control and dominate nature, rather than trying to understand and harmonize with the forces of nature. As I listen to Rahul, it is obvious to me that our obsession with economic growth has driven our systems toward a ruthless exploitation of nature and natural resources."

She calmed down a little and looked at me.

She then spoke with a sense of disappointment: "Aparna, we now face most disturbing results due to all of this. You can see, for example, serious environmental degradation due to air and water pollution, nuclear waste and massive deforestation, and extinction of innumerable varieties of fauna, flora and species. We now face an alarming ecological imbalance which is showing up as global warming, melting polar ice caps, depletion of ozone layers and increasing radiation hazards. I do not know how much worse it is going to get, before we wake up to the reality."

I knew that Neera had been a student of philosophy for her Master's degree.

So, I asked her: "Neera, I see your point. But let me ask you, if the economic systems are unable to help, could we turn to religion and philosophy to guide us to the right path?"

She responded with a feeling of frustration in her voice: "I wish it was possible to do so. Unfortunately, religions have divided mankind, instead of uniting them in a common bond of human values. There is so much fighting in the name of religion. What is even worse, when the fundamentalist positions of different religious groups are mixed with violence, they show up in the most sinister form of terrorism. I think, the less said on this, the better."

She continued: "As for the social systems, you can see that the rat-race for material success and insatiable greed for money and power, have left everything else behind. The entire social system is seriously compromised by corruption at various levels."

She paused, and then said: "All this vitally affects each one of us. At the level of an individual, these forces have led to disruption of families, and problems of alienation and drug abuse. All these show up as growing frustration and conflict within an individual. Consequent stress becomes a part of one's life, and many stress-related health problems both at the physical and mental level, pose a serious challenge to one's well-being and happiness."

This situation looked quite bad. All of us were listening, and trying to think of some possible solution to the problems pointed out by her.

I wondered, 'What about the judicial and political systems? Surely, they could be expected to help'.

I looked at Raj and he seemed to have read my thoughts.

He spoke rather slowly: "I can say that the courts of law are doing their best, but they have their limitations. Basically, our judicial system and rule of law provide the means for enforcement of rights and for resolution of disputes at all levels – personal, collective and social. They also enforce the system of checks and balances on the exercise of executive and legislative powers by the State and its various organs. But the judicial system in our country is suffering from a serious overload and lack of resources and our judicial process continues to be burdened by complex, long drawn and unwieldy procedures. Unfortunately, all this has resulted in inordinate delays at all levels of the judicial process. Nevertheless, you can see how our Supreme Court has pushed forward many critical reforms and solutions which were otherwise more or less given up as lost causes. For example, so much has been possible only by judicial intervention of the courts, in the area of pollution control, ecological and environmental protection, and more recently, the fight against corruption."

He paused for a moment, and then added: "However, generally speaking, the judicial system can resolve only a specific dispute or situation of conflict, and does not do much to remove the underlying cause of the conflict. The basic contradictions in the social or economic systems remain untouched and the conflict inherent therein continues unabated."

There was a long silence. The conversation this whole

afternoon was quite depressing for all of us. We all needed a break and some rest, and also time to think more about what we had discussed. Hopefully, we could find some answers if we continued our search.

We went back to our rooms for some well-deserved rest. I relaxed for a while, and then Raj and I came out into the balcony of our room to have tea. It was getting cold out there and we put on our warm clothing. Soon after we finished tea, Raj went back to the room to attend to his email.

As I was sitting in the balcony and quietly watching the natural beauty of mountains and clouds washed in the soft light of the setting sun, I became aware of my own state of existence at that time. I could see my present moment of existence as a link between my past and my future, all flowing in time. As we move with the flow of time, we do realize occasionally that our life is so precious and there is so much potential for developing many facets of our existence and experiencing them in the glory of their richness, diversity and unity. Our life is so full of promise for joy, happiness and harmony both at our physical and emotional levels. The nature around us also appears so full of beauty and charm. If we open up ourselves to nature, we can experience that beauty and charm everywhere, all the time – in the splendid glory of a sunrise, quiet dignity of a sunset, sun-splashed beaches, moon-lit nights, flowers and trees dancing in the rain, clouds floating in the sky, and rivers flowing like music.

But a question cropped up in my mind. How much of this joy, happiness and harmony does actually get assimilated in our living experience? We see all of it out there, but we never seem to be able to reach out and assimilate it in our own life and existence. Instead, we find ourselves caught in a situation where we are almost completely preoccupied in coping with the systems in which we live and work – our social, economic and political systems, which not only get more and more complex but remain continually in a state of conflict. These vitally affect our existence, and keep us tied down into a kind of battle for survival. And then, the world around us looks rather unfriendly – in an environment of fierce competition and various pressures pulling us in different directions.

While I was lost in my thoughts, time was running. Soon, it was time to meet Rahul and Neera at dinner. We dressed up and left for the dining hall.

DINNER TURNED OUT TO BE VERY pleasant and enjoyable. We had very good company, and Neera had herself gone to the kitchen earlier to help the chef prepare something special for us. We later discovered that she had herself prepared two lovely dishes and a delicious dessert pudding. She had found out about our wedding anniversary and wanted us to have something special for dinner that evening. We just loved that.

And, there was so much to talk at the dinner table about all that was happening in our lives. Some times, I notice that when husband and wife are together on their own, not much conversation goes on between them – more so when they have been married for 15 years or more, like we were at that time! But when good friends join, things change and conversation becomes lively, full of laughter, and practically never-ending. Real friendship, I thought, was such a precious gift in our lives.

After dinner, we moved into the lounge next to the dining hall. As the evening temperature had fallen below six degrees centigrade, the hotel staff had lighted the fireplace in the lounge. The glow and warmth of the fire had made the place quite cozy and comfortable.

The dancing flames in the fireplace looked so beautiful and reminded me of the flames on oil lamps which I had seen during the lecture I had attended in the Ashram in Rishikesh. My mind quietly pictured these flames as fields of energy, radiating from the fireplace and spreading out in all directions. I had a distinct sensation of touching and connecting with them, and that felt so good, almost like a warm handshake with them.

As we were having dessert and coffee, we went back to our earlier discussion that afternoon.

Neera volunteered to speak first, and said: "I have thought about what we have been discussing this afternoon. It seems to me, we need to be clear about the root cause of all the conflict, which we find everywhere. I think the present situation is due to fragmentation in our own lives and in the world around us at every level. We have broken down and divided everything in parts, and in the process, we have lost our ability to see the things in their holistic dimension. We just see the bits and pieces and fail to see the total picture."

I asked her: "Neera, you may be right, but what has that got to do with the problem of conflicts that we talked about?"

She sounded quite knowledgeable on the subject as she spoke: "Aparna, you are a medical doctor, so you may already know this. But let me point out that division of whole into parts has at least two significant consequences. One, the characteristics and qualities referable to the wholeness are lost. Two, the inter-relationships between the parts when considered separately, differ from their inter-relationships as constituents of the whole."

All of us were listening attentively.

She spoke slowly, in carefully chosen words: "The first consequence follows from the premise that the whole is more than the sum of its parts. The second point arises because the overall purpose at the level of whole may differ from that at the level of each part. Let me give you some examples. Take the example of water. Qualities of water arise from the combination of its constituents – two molecules of hydrogen and one molecule of oxygen; and these qualities can not be found in any of these molecules when considered separately. Similarly, the chemical constituents of sugar do not by themselves have the sweetness present in sugar. Sweetness emerges only when all these are integrated into the wholeness of a crystal of sugar."

She paused, as if to wait for a question.

This was getting quite interesting and we wanted her to continue, and she did: "Take for example what I am just now speaking to you. A sentence, when broken down into words would lose the meaning which arises from its syntax and structure of the collection of words together. A word when broken down into its constituent alphabets would lose its meaning altogether. Essentially, therefore, the structure and pattern of inter-relationships between the constituents are defined and determined by certain unique properties of the whole as distinguished from its parts."

She looked at our faces, some of which had a blank look. She realized that we needed more explanation.

Trying to help, she added slowly: "Please understand that the inter-relationships between the parts, when viewed not in isolation but as joining together as elements of the whole, are unified in their purpose – by the purpose of the whole. This means that these inter-relationships are integrated and inter-dependent, and not competitive and conflicting. On the contrary, when the whole is broken down and divided into parts or segments, the structure and pattern underlying the whole get lost. The divided parts then no longer function according to a common unifying principle. Other influences and forces at work then drive them to a different set of relationships which are not consistent with the concept and purpose of the whole. This leads to fragmentation, and fragmentation results in conflict. Today, we seem to have fragmented our world, our lives and our own selves – and that appears to be the genesis of conflict in which we are caught."

I looked at Neera with clear admiration in my eyes, for the depth of her knowledge and her insight as she explained the basic cause of our conflict.

But I did not know what to say or do, except to order another round of coffee for all of us.

As we were trying to focus on our cups of coffee, our minds were busy absorbing the impact of all that Neera had said. She sounded so sure of what she said and it was difficult for us to disagree.

Rahul probably took the cue and decided to speak: "I think she has a point. As I see it, our economic world is fragmented into classes and categories, and unfortunately, all of them have opposing economic interests. That inevitably results in constant ongoing conflicts among them. Our social systems are split and divided by race, religion and caste, and the political situation around the world is divided by blocks and divisions made on the basis of conflicting military and economic interests."

He continued: "Even at our personal level, our own lives

seem fragmented by our conflicting positions as individuals, and as members of a family, society or nation. Our roles and goals in each of these positions do not seem to be in harmony with one another.

Sometimes, I feel that we are being torn apart by the conflicting pulls and pressures of the systems in which we have to live and work. Not surprisingly, I get confused and frustrated by the conflicting signals coming from the social and economic notions of growth and success expected of me in the material world, and on the other hand, contradictory signals coming to me from the philosophical, religious and ethical systems which seek to give direction to my life. I do not know which one is right – and quite often, I just live with a nagging doubt and skepticism arising from the sheer elusiveness of happiness and fulfillment in our lives."

This was really too bad. If an intelligent and successful economist like Rahul felt like that, we could be much worse off.

"But why don't they correct what is wrong?" I asked. Rahul came forward with his analysis as an economist.

He said: "This is the problem. Sound economic theory must cover all the participants in the economic process, namely, owners and managers, producers and workers, consumers and other interest groups, on the basis that each of these classes are integral components of a unified whole. Instead of doing that, our economic theory has split and divided their respective spheres, even though each of them is expected to work together in a unified manner for a successful economic result."

I was listening with full attention, but I was not sure if I fully understood what he was trying to say.

I asked him: "Rahul, this sounds very interesting. But can

you explain, how does this affect us, and how does this result in the situation of conflict that we are discussing?"

Rahul responded: "Ok. Let me give you the full picture. This may sound strange, but economic analysis has divided the economic process into segments, such as production, consumption, distribution, etc. and each of these is dealt with in isolation from the rest. In this fragmented approach, their close inter-dependence is disregarded, and we overlook the fact that each segment supports the other, and in turn, is conditioned by the other. For example, production depends upon consumption, and vice versa, and the economics of distribution affects and conditions the economics of consumption and production. It is obvious that an individual engaged in a production process is simultaneously also a consumer. His choices as a consumer – and the economic factors guiding those choices –is not only closely inter-linked but are inter-dependent with his position in the process of distribution which determines his income and wealth levels. But strangely enough, the economics of distribution has been totally segregated from the others, and has been virtually left out of the economics of production, consumption and exchange. That is the main reason why the economic growth remains non-inclusive, does not reach society as a whole, and despite all claims of economic growth, poverty of the masses continues unabated."

He then proceeded to explain how this situation results in conflict within the economic sphere.

He continued: "As you can expect in such a situation, our economic and regulatory policy framework deals with economic relationships and the markets and other mechanisms intended to regulate these relationships, but this is done only in reference to a particular segment of economic process and not the whole. The various participants in the economic process continue to have conflicting objectives and the economic model does not provide a unified common goal or strategy for them. For instance, business and industry are driven and judged by the profit criterion, and maximization of profit is taken as the measure of their success. However, it is obvious that profit maximization as an objective function is defined and becomes relevant basically from the standpoint of those who have provided capital. This is of little interest as far as the workers or consumers are concerned. This has automatically led to confrontation between capital and labor, and producers and consumers, and has placed them in opposing positions in a class struggle in a Marxist sense. It is unfortunate that such class struggle does not remain confined to the economic domain, but becomes an unavoidable feature of the overall social and political existence of people, and that leads to conflict pervading all walks of life."

I had never looked at the problem of conflict from this perspective. Having listened to Rahul, I now understood the genesis of conflict in the economic sphere.

Raj seemed to agree with this, and said: "Rahul, I am not an economist, but I am also disappointed with the situation as it exists today. I can see that rapid industrialization led by science and technology has resulted in massive growth of wealth and economic power. But I am disappointed to find that while there has been a clear upward shift in the levels of overall production and consumption, the absence of corresponding development in the distribution function of economics has led to growing disparities in income levels and a worsening concentration of economic power. All this shows up in continuing conflicts at various levels."

He paused a little, and then added in a sad tone: "As if this was not bad enough, rampant corruption has entered at all levels of our economic and political process. I just do not know how things can be changed."

I was still wondering. I had always thought that science can solve all our problems. Why not this problem of conflict?

I wanted to explore this, and asked: "All right, but science has brought about so much development into our lives. And science proceeds on logic and rationality. Can we not look to science to solve this problem as well?"

Neera was the one who responded: "I hope that can be done. But it does not seem likely at present, because science itself has been working on a fragmented model of our material world and our own body and mind. In fact, it seems to me that this scientific view point is what has resulted in our fragmented perception of ourselves and the world around us."

This was quite a shocking statement. How can science be wrong, and how can we blame science for the fragmentation and consequent conflict in our existence? I hoped Neera knew what she was saying.

She did seem to know, as she continued: "If you look at the development of classical physics through the last three centuries, you will see that the foundation for the impressive growth of science and technology was laid by the renowned 17th century scientist Sir Isaac Newton. Before that, the famous French philosopher Rene Descartes had already provided the framework for materialist philosophy, which later became the basis for scientific knowledge and progress. Descartes separated mind from matter and called all matter including the human body as 'res-extensa', which meant reality extending in the outside world and totally separate from the mind. This introduced a subject-object dualism – the mind as the subject-observer called 'res-cogitans', and the external world as the observed-object called 'res-extensa'. This separation of mind and matter, as two separate realities, became a fundamental premise of the later materialist philosophy."

She continued: "Equally important was the analytical framework provided by Descartes, which became known in the following centuries as the Cartesian framework, and was eminently successful in scientific research and development during that period. His analytical framework proceeded on the basis of breaking down complex phenomena into pieces and understanding it by studying the properties of the divided parts. This was reinforced by Galileo who was a great astronomer, mathematician and philosopher in early 17th century. He provided a mathematical basis for measuring the properties of matter, that is, mass and motion, and he held that only quantitative data and information provided the basis for knowledge. Galileo's staunch quantitative approach provided an objective and independently verifiable basis for scientific enquiry and knowledge. At the same time, it excluded all subjective experience as unacceptable in scientific knowledge, and also excluded all other characteristics like human thoughts, emotions, ethics, religion, art, culture, and other qualitative aspects and values in life. This approach was later known as the reductionist approach in material philosophy."

She was obviously enjoying this – like a teacher giving lesson to her students, and more so while we were listening to her as very attentive students.

She continued: "Newton adopted this reductionist approach with remarkable success for providing a mechanical model for explaining the working of the universe. He portrayed the universe as a huge machine, which works perfectly like a clock; and this is driven by infallible mechanical laws of motion which operate in a space-time dimension. He evolved a set of differential equations to explain all motion of solid bodies, and these are popularly known as Newtonian mechanics. Newtonian concepts very well explained the mass; motion and inter-relationships between the various parts of the great machine of the universe, and these became the foundation for scientific knowledge in the following centuries. Starting from the times of Newton, the reductionist approach was and continues to be regarded as the appropriate basis for all scientific knowledge."

"All this went on very well for the next three centuries. During the 20th century, the world of science saw new developments in quantum physics. Since then, there has been a growing recognition of the limitations of classical reductionist approach. Let me mention just three of these," Neera said.

"First: This approach ignores the unifying principle underlying the whole. Consequently, it fails to recognize certain essential features of the whole, such as inter-dependence, coordination and coherence between the constituent elements.

Second: Since the reductionist approach focuses only on a particular segment, many significant aspects external to that segment are ignored even though these are otherwise important. This leads to a fragmented and incomplete viewpoint, which is inadequate and inappropriate. For instance, the current economic and social systems focus on a segmented view at the level of an economic entity, and hence leave out externalities like social costs, ecological and environmental issues, despite their acknowledged relevance and significance.

Third: This approach leaves out aspects, which are

considered non-quantifiable under the conventional measurement system. The whole exercise then becomes mechanical and fails to integrate the ethical, emotional, cultural and other qualitative aspects of our well-being and existence."

She then added: "We need to correct all this by adopting a holistic approach instead of relying upon the reductionist approach. It appears that quantum physics has opened up the way to do that now."

I was reminded about the reference to recent developments in quantum physics during my earlier conversation with Dr. Sonali at the Ashram in Rishikesh.

When I mentioned this to Neera, she nodded in the affirmative and said: "This was the position all along in classical physics. However, we have recently seen the new developments in quantum physics which have changed the world-view of science in a very fundamental way. The classical physics deals with matter and energy at the level where we actually see or experience them directly with our senses, and this is popularly referred to in science as the classical or macro-level view. On the other hand, quantum physics deals with particles and energy at the sub-atomic level, that is, at the level below the molecules and atoms, which until then were believed to be the smallest constituents of matter. At the quantum level, the reality looks very different."

I complimented Neera, and said: "Neera, I never imagined that you could give us such a good lesson in science, and also make it so interesting. But we are discussing the problem of conflict in our world, and I am still trying to find out how we can use all this knowledge for that purpose. You have said that Newtonian physics and Cartesian philosophy have resulted in fragmentation. Would you say that quantum physics can lead the way to unification?"

Neera got excited at this invitation from me, and quickly replied: "You are absolutely right. This is what is happening already. I don't think I can tell you all about quantum physics, but surely, it has brought us much closer to our reality in a truly holistic perspective. As I mentioned earlier, classical science had divided and analyzed everything in terms of atoms and their proton, neutron and electrons. All these were understood to be solid material objects and unconnected components of matter and energy. Quantum physics has shown that it is quantum energy, which is at work at the most basic level of all these phenomena. And it is quantum energy that inter-connects everything that exists anywhere, including all of us. We are all inter-connected at the quantum level, and therefore, we affect each other, howsoever subtle and miniscule the effect may be. According to new knowledge of quantum physics, we are all one, and the notion of separate existence is more an illusion than a reality."

She was obviously happy to note our interest in the subject. Encouraged by our attention, she further elaborated: "Quantum physics can give us a perfect scientific holistic model of our reality and existence. The model can be based upon the findings of quantum physics, which are scientifically proven and can be verified on an objective basis. It is very interesting to realize that this holistic view now emerging from quantum physics is identical to the view of our reality and existence as understood and described in our ancient scriptures. This is indeed remarkable. I am very hopeful that this convergence of scientific and spiritual knowledge will establish a holistic model on the basis of which our social, economic and political systems can be redesigned, and the conflicts arising from their present deficiencies can be eliminated. I can see that we have now found a bridge between science and spirituality and it is now possible to take a unified view of our existence both from a scientific and spiritual perspective."

I was greatly impressed, and could not help speaking out: "This is music to my ears. I have always felt so frustrated trying to reconcile what science tells me about me and this world, and what the scriptures tell me about my spiritual identity. They always seem so far apart – and one virtually rejects the other. I never know which one to accept and live by. Neera, I would be the happiest person, if what you now say is true."

Neera responded: "Yes, Aparna, this is true, but don't accept my word for it. I will give you a few books from some of the greatest scientists of this century, including those who are founders of quantum physics, and have won Nobel prizes for their great contributions in this field of knowledge."

We never realized how quickly time had passed. It was getting close to midnight. We knew that Rahul and Neera planned to leave early next morning. But at our request, and also probably due to their own interest in continuing the discussion on this subject, they postponed their departure to the next evening. I felt quite happy that we would see them at breakfast next morning, and possibly be able to bring our discussion to a more meaningful level.

THE NEXT MORNING after breakfast, we moved into the lounge, and Neera picked up our conversation from the previous evening.

She said: "We have talked about fragmentation as the cause

of our conflicts. Let me show you what has been said about this by some of the greatest writers of today."

Then, she read out the following passage written by Fritjof Capra in his book 'The Web of Life': "The power of abstract thinking has led us to treat the natural environment – the web of life – as if it consisted of separate parts, to be exploited by different interest groups. Moreover, we have extended this fragmented view to our human society, dividing it into different nations, races, religious and political groups. The belief that all these fragments – in themselves, in our environment, and in our society – are really separate, has alienated us from nature and from our fellow human beings, and thus has diminished us."[20]

She sounded totally convinced, and went on to express her own thoughts: "This is the state of our existence today. If we don't realize, it is only because in the process of fragmentation, we have lost our focus and cannot clearly see the reality. Our notion of our own self has become quite hazy, and we are living in this world almost half-awake – with a blurred vision, as if in a mist or fog."

And then she became emotional, and added: "Out there, around us, there does exist a living and vibrant world, but due to our fragmented vision we are unable to grasp the full picture, and we are left with a very limited and hazy view of all that life has to offer. Things become even more difficult when there is so much change-taking place in the world, at such a fast pace as never before. We seem to be living in 'a transient society' as pointed out by Alvin Toffler in his book 'Future Shock'."

She had become quite charged, as she went on: "All the time, we are in a fast-forward mode, and our existence has become transient, fleeting and momentary, where things quickly pass by and the identity of self vanishes into a crowd of non-descript, non-identifiable and faceless entities."

With a sense of frustration in her voice, she added: "In such a state of fragmentation, how can we see clearly, and how can we hear legibly?"

She paused, took a deep breath, and trying to sound positive, said: "Life in this world has all the colors with a variety of shades and emotions, but these can be appreciated only when we see the full picture. Life has all the music, with the melody, the rhythm, and the harmony, but these can be experienced only in their unified wholeness. In our present state of existence, we see only a fragmented part of the picture which fails to convey the meaning; we hear only a part of the music which appears as disjointed bits and pieces of sound – only noise, not the music."

She did not conceal her frustration, and her voice reflected her mental agony: "Fragmentation and the consequent conflict have entered our psyche; and deep down in our minds, we carry long shadows of conflict and insecurity in our lives. They are always overshadowing our vision and our sensitivities. Everything appears conditioned by a notion of conflict, and our responses, our strategies and our systems now evolve on that basis. It seems that conflict has become a reality of our lives and an integral part of our existence. It is an irony of fate that even while fighting it, we are only perpetuating the conflict rather than removing it. The more we fight, the more we get involved."

We were touched by her words.

I looked at Rahul. Maybe he had an answer.

He took over from Neera, and said: "I have also given this a lot of thought. A little bit of reflection would show that basically the problem is not with the world as God created it, but the problem is with the relationships superimposed by us through the socio-economic systems designed and created by us, and our ways of dealing with them."

He added: "In order to fully understand the situation, we need to ask ourselves some fundamental questions: Do we see ourselves as an integral part of the universe, or as a separate self? Are we seeking harmony, or do we want to dominate and control everything around us? Are we playing a zero-sum game, where we always want us to win and everyone else to lose – not just once or twice, but every time? Do we assume that we can do that, and have a right to do that?"

We kept listening, as Rahul continued: "If we do not like the answers to these questions, then we must consciously ask ourselves: Do we seek to discover the reality of our own self, and experience the full potential of our life in every moment of our existence? Do we wish to live not in a state of conflict, but in the joy and the glory of being one with the entire universe?"

He paused, and then added: "Undoubtedly, we can discover our selves, and live in such cosmic unity – says the Vedanta philosophy – if we take a holistic approach to our existence."

To reinforce what he said, he asked Neera to read out the following sentence from the same book written by Fritj of Capra: "To regain our full humanity, we have to regain our experience of connectedness with the entire web of life."

Neera also mentioned that a similar thought has been echoed by David Bohm – another eminent scientist of this era, who was a co-founder of quantum physics and was honored with the Nobel prize for his work.

She read out from a book written by David Bohm to show that he also points out the futility of the "fragmentary western approach" and recommends the adoption of "Eastern notions" which include not only "a worldview that denies division and fragmentation" but also "techniques of meditation that lead the whole process of mental operation non-verbally to the sort of quiet state of orderly and smooth flow needed to end fragmentation both in the actual process of thought and its content." [21]

My mind instantly went back to the lecture I had heard from Swami Ji at the Ashram in Rishikesh, which told me what the scriptures have said. Now I also knew what the great scientists have said.

I felt truly blessed, and had a distinct feeling that science and spirituality were sending me the same message to show me the path ahead in my life.

THE MORNING HAD PASSED in our discussion and soon it was time for lunch. Our post-lunch afternoon session was short as Rahul and Neera were driving down and wanted to leave before sunset.

I was keen to know what they thought about possible solutions on these issues. So, I asked: "I think, we all know our problem. We also realize that the source of conflict is in the economic and social systems within which we have to live and work. The obvious question is 'what can be done about this'?"

Rahul thought for a while, and then answered: "The first thing to do is to recognize our inter-connectivity at the most fundamental level with everything, every person, and every other form of life in the world. I think, there can be no debate on this, after we understand our scriptures on Vedanta philosophy and know what quantum physics has found. Once we accept that, our social and economic systems should follow a truly holistic approach – and must move away from fragmentation of our existence and from our adversarial relationships created due to that fragmentation."

He wanted to further elaborate, and said: "All these systems should be guided by a pragmatic approach based upon an objective function with which everybody can identify oneself. Such an objective function should explicitly aim to achieve enrichment of our existence at all levels and in all facets including the qualitative aspects of life. These need to be defined in terms of creation or addition of certain values, both economic and social, which are shared by all and not only by a particular interest group."

He added: "As you know, an individual strives to achieve those values in life that society recognizes as parameters of success. Each one of us can then genuinely work in our daily lives for such value addition – to our material world, to our social fabric, and to our environment. It is necessary that these systems should not only focus on creation and measurement of the defined values, but must also ensure that the results are shared equitably on the basis of the contributions to the value added. That would work as a pragmatic framework for all our activity, and would open up the best opportunity for each one of us to put forward our very best and realize our full potential in life."

Raj wanted a clarification: "It looks fine as a concept at the macro level. But in our day-to-day work, we are operating at the micro level, where we need to focus and work on a specific issue within an analytical framework, or where we have to handle an inter-personal relationship at the individual level. How does that work from a holistic viewpoint?"

Rahul responded affirmatively, and said: "Yes, that is important. Otherwise, all this would remain good just in theory. I must therefore, clarify that the holistic approach does not question the practical necessity for classification and categorization of things in parts, nor does it question the need for sub-systems. What it requires is that all of these must be designed and viewed on the basis of the dynamics of the whole. The concept of wholeness must remain the fundamental principle at each level of the system, and at each level of classification and categorization of things or our relationships in the world. This will enable us to evolve a unified network, a kind of web of inter-relationships amongst all the classes, constituents and system levels."

I was trying to grasp the meaning of what Rahul was telling us, and I wanted to ask for a clarification, but he looked so confident that we kept quiet.

Neera sensed this, and came forward with an explanation: "Ok. Let me give a very simple example just to explain what he has in mind. Look at me. I am an individual, and when I say 'I am Neera', I am referring to myself as an individual in my own right. But if I look at myself as 'Neera Chawla', I recognize my position as a member or constituent of the 'Chawla' family; and then my relationships with other members of the family, and my many rights and obligations as a member of that family become apparent. Similarly, if I recognize myself as a Hindu, or as an Indian, all my relationships in those contexts also become relevant to the way I need to think and act. In a sense, I become a part of the whole at each such level, and not just a part in isolation."

I found this explanation quite helpful for me to understand the basic idea.

I wanted her to continue, and she did: "You can appreciate that if I define my relationships, rights and obligations in isolation as an individual, these would be very different from those which arise when I recognize myself in a larger perspective of wholeness of which I am a part. It would also be obvious that unless such wholeness conditions my relationships and thoughts, conflicts would arise when I have to deal with, or relate to, the other parts of the same whole. The position can get worse, if each member of the family sees and treats himself or herself as an isolated individual rather than a component of the whole, and therefore, does not structure his or her relationships by reference to the dynamics and conditions of the whole. For instance, if a young person in the family disregards the fact that he is part of the larger family, and considers himself only as a separate individual, relationships would get strained and conflicts would arise when it comes to the interests and values of the family as a whole."

"Wow!" I said: "Neera, I will be very careful in describing myself from now onwards. Always, I must say I am 'Aparna Gupta', not just 'Aparna'. I thought 'Gupta' got added to my name because of Raj, but now I know what it means. So if I am also 'Gupta', there would be no conflict between me and Raj. How wonderful!"

Raj smiled, and said: "I hope this works. Good solution to our problems."

Turning to Rahul, I wanted to know in more specific terms about the implications of the holistic approach for our systems.

It was getting late, but he was good enough to sum up his thoughts: "A holistic approach implies a new paradigm and a consequent shift of values and strategies in our systems – from dualistic to non-dualistic, and from reductionism to holistic. This would mean that instead of analysis, we would rely upon synthesis in our approach to problems and their solutions. Instead of abstraction, our thinking would focus on integration. In pursuit of

our economic activity, we would recognize and value inter-dependence, instead of competition. In our personal relationships, we would seek harmony instead of domination. And in our work place, we would adopt networking instead of structures of hierarchy."

He further elaborated: "In this new paradigm, the guiding principles and assumptions for our economic, social and political systems will be derived from the fundamental concept of unity. In each field, this will have to be worked out by the experts in that field. I am only an economist, and so let me point out just three basic principles we would follow for designing our economic system: One, unity of economic process; two, unity of participants; three, unity of purpose."

He continued: "Let me also briefly explain how each of these would work. Unity of economic process would call for an economic theory that would fully integrate production, consumption, exchange and distribution functions on the basis of their inter-relationships, rather than taking a segmented approach for one or the other of these functions. In particular, distribution would have to be included as an integral and essential part of the economic process – and its close inter-dependence with other functions of production and consumption would have to be explicitly recognized."

"The principle of unity of participants would require full integration of the interests of all the players in the economic process – capital, labor, producer, consumer, government and the public at large – and not just one, or some of them."

"Unity of purpose would require adoption of an objective function that everyone can share and work for. The present concept of profit-maximization fails on this principle, and therefore, this may be replaced by a concept of sustainable economic development based upon maximization of 'value-added'. This value-added concept would provide a common basis for all the participants to work together and share the results."

He continued: "All this would mean that business and industry would plan for, and be judged by, the total value-added and not by the profit for a specific select group. Appropriate accounting and measurement framework will be evolved for the measurement and quantification of value-added, and that would recognize and include all relevant costs and benefits – whether internal or external to an enterprise, whether monetary or otherwise, and whether quantitative or qualitative."

It became clear to me that this was the holistic vision for our future systems and this was the way forward to eliminate the conflicts we were talking about. Rahul and Neera had articulated that so well. It was for us to think, and act upon it.

We hugged them and said good-bye as they got into their car. It was such a wonderful coincidence that they came over when we were there. I would never forget the time we spent with them in those lovely surroundings. Our discussions with them are still fresh in my memory.

RAJ AND I HAD A LIGHT DINNER, and thereafter we went back to our room.

There was so much we had discussed during the last two days with Rahul and Neera about the causes of conflict in the world around us. But I still had some unanswered questions.

As we settled down in our room, I told Raj: "Talking to Rahul and Neera has helped me a lot. I think I now have a much better idea why we are having so much conflict in the world and in our own lives. I now realize that if we want to solve this problem, our economic and social systems need to be based upon a holistic model as explained so well by Rahul. But changing these systems would take a long time and this will require a dedicated action by our leaders. Raj, do you think that can happen?"

Raj responded: "Of course, that can happen. Everything changes – and the systems can also evolve toward a holistic model. But in order for this to happen, the first thing is that everyone must understand how we have gone wrong due to our fragmented approach. Once we realize that, we need to understand the holistic model as described by Rahul and Neera. Only then we can take the necessary action at the collective level. Our political leaders, policy makers and economists will have to lead that."

Then he added: "Therefore, we have to articulate the thinking process of everyone, and spread these ideas so that a consensus can emerge and action can follow. This needs to happen first at the top level where policies are made and decisions are taken."

He then continued, to explain this further: "As you know, I am a member of the management boards of several big corporations. Let me tell you, there are very distinguished and experienced persons who are directors on these boards. If they understand and accept the holistic model explained by Rahul, this can change the way things are done down the line within the organization. If the word 'holistic' sounds too abstract, you may understand it as 'unified'. A unified approach will harmonize the interests of all those concerned with the corporation and its business, and conflicts will be avoided at all levels."

I was curious, and asked: "If there are such competent persons to guide us, why does this unified approach not happen? Surely, they know all this – like the situation being created in my hospital. Why don't they do something about it?"

Raj replied in his usual cautious tone: "Yes, you are right. They should do something about it. Unfortunately, they often do not take the initiative. Many times, the owners have already made up their minds, and others just take the path of least resistance, and go along with that. I think the decision-makers as well as their advisors have a great responsibility to correct this situation. They need to be proactive and ensure proper policy and decision-making on such important matters."

I did not know what to say about this situation.

He thought for a while and then added: "Aparna, the overall situation is not difficult to handle. We have so much young talent now coming into business, industry and services. This young generation is highly talented and motivated. They are working at all levels and are capable of achieving the targets in the best possible manner. I can say from my own knowledge and experience that wherever the top management has given them a clear-cut policy with quick and firm decisions and the necessary freedom to act, they have performed very well. You can see that happening in many corporations in the infrastructure as well as service sectors. I have full hope and confidence that as they take the center-stage, they will move the systems toward a unified approach. A much more efficient and harmonious environment will then become possible for us to live and work in."

I was happy to hear this, but I pointed out: "Good to know that this is possible. But left to myself, I find myself too small a person to change the situation as it exists today. I am just a doctor, and you are just a lawyer – two individuals trying to cope with life as it is. No, we are too small to bring about a change in these systems."

Adding a positive note, I said: "Yes, we can do our bit by spreading the knowledge and supporting the change process. But for the time being I need to know that while I wait for the systems to change for the better, what is there that I can do at my own personal level? What can I do to save me from the unhappiness being created by all this ongoing conflict in the world around me? We need to know and focus upon what you and I can do in the present situation?"

Raj held my hand, and said: "Aparna, don't worry. We will find out what to do, and will do that. Let us think about that. Right now, you need some rest."

Raj had received some legal documents in his email that required his urgent attention. He got busy on them. Since I didn't want to disturb him when he was on his important work, I came out and sat in the balcony.

The atmosphere all around was very peaceful yet invigorating. I closed my eyes and within a few minutes I was in a state of complete relaxation. Gently, I slipped into my meditation.

My meditation went on beautifully, and I share my experience as follows. If you like, you can experience it yourself in a peaceful place.

"Om... Om... Om..."

I SEE MY BODY. Still and calm. It is here. Still and calm. I feel my body. Still and calm.

I feel the energy flowing in the body. Soft sensations of energy flow. I feel those in my feet and my toes. Moving up, I feel them in my legs, in my back, in my stomach, in my chest, in my throat, in my eyebrows, and then in the crown of my head.

Now I feel a shaft of energy moving up my spine to my Crown Chakra at the top of my head. I feel soft tingling sensations on the spine – moving up to the back of my head. My whole being is now an energy field – extending in and around my body. I can sense its very subtle vibrations all over.

I am energy personified. My whole body is energy in a highly condensed form and seen as matter. I can feel that matter as vibrating and pulsating energy – very subtle and very smooth vibrations. I become aware of my entire energy field. This is me – my true self. This is my consciousness field, and everything exists in this field.

My whole being is filled up with a soft glow of light. As I become aware of this, it becomes brighter and brighter. It is a field of light spreading out in all directions. I am that light field, in and around my body, and pulsating ever so smoothly.

My physical body has slowly dissolved in it. My awareness of myself is now one with that light field. I feel it expanding. There is light above and around, a vast expanse of light, extending everywhere, into the sky, beyond the horizon, beyond that in limitless space. I can feel it as a bright cosmic light field extending in all directions without any boundaries.

My light field is rising, and now connecting with this vast cosmic light field. Slowly, it merges. I am now free and floating. I have merged into the cosmic light field. Now I am that cosmic light field, a vast expanse, everywhere, without any boundaries. I have no limits. I am one with the cosmic field of light – my consciousness is one with cosmic consciousness. There is no beginning, no end.

I can see the world down below, as if I am looking at it from outer space. It is so clear, and it looks so beautiful. I am enjoying this panoramic view of the world. I see a vast multitude of figures in it moving, some slowly, some whizzing past. I see movement all over. I see everything in constant motion as if driven by some invisible force. I become aware of the order and coherence of all the movements, as if everything is linked to everything else. I become aware of their harmony and synchronicity, and their cyclical movement without any visible beginning or end.

I feel my own subtle presence in this universe of things and their movements, and I feel a secure comfort in flowing with their flow. It is effortless and so peaceful. I see that everything howsoever big or small, is in it, and is moving along in harmony. I see everything moving at its own pace, as a thing, and simultaneously also within the movement of all the things combined and moving together.

I now see beyond this view of the world. I can now see

many planets in our solar system, each planet moving in its orbit at its own pace. I can see all of them moving together collectively as a group, as part of the solar system, in complete synchronicity and unity. It is a beautiful view of all the planets moving in perfect harmony.

I look beyond the moving planets and I see the space around them. I become aware of the vast space spread out everywhere. I sense its infinite expanse, without any beginning, without any end, and so peaceful. I become aware of the glow and I feel very subtle sensations in the space. I see very tiny flashes of light twinkling in it all over. They are so soft and subtle. I sense this vast space as a living and vibrating energy field. I become aware that all planets, stars, our earth, and everything else, are within this field. I have a vivid sense of infinity – a cosmic energy field spread out everywhere, without any boundary, or beginning or end.

In the synchronized movements of everything happening within this infinite field, I am seeing the cosmic dance of Shiva, the lord of all cosmic energy, creation and dissolution. In the melodious harmony and rhythm of these movements, I am hearing the symphony of cosmic music.

I am one with the Eternal. I am in perfect bliss and eternal peace.

"Shivo-ham… Shivo-ham… Shivo-ham…"

That pure cosmic consciousness – That is me.

I REMAINED IN THAT blissful state, until Raj came out into the balcony and sat beside me.

I wanted to tell him that I had not only discovered myself but had also moved beyond the realms of conflict in this world – at least for those few moments.

But, I kept quiet.

CHAPTER 3

What to do?

WHEN WE GOT BACK to our home in New Delhi after a memorable holiday in Anandipur, both of us got very busy in our work. I could not do much of reading, but I did manage to find time everyday for my meditation.

The following week we were invited to Founder's Day function at Modern School. Our son Varun was studying there in Class VI. This annual function was an important event to which all parents were invited. As part of the evening's program, the students had planned to present a 20-minute play and Varun was playing a leading part. This was all the more reason for both of us to be there that evening.

This school was one of the most prestigious schools in the city, and the arrangements for the function were done with great care for decor and elegance. Air Chief Marshall OP Mehra was invited as the Chief Guest. He had a most illustrious career, and besides his highest rank and position at the helm of the country's air force, he had held the prestigious position as Governors of Maharashtra, and later on of Rajasthan. Apart from his extensive knowledge and wisdom, he commanded great respect for his high standards of discipline, integrity and patriotism. He was able to inspire the air force personnel at all levels with these qualities and led them with great distinction during some of the most challenging times faced by the country during the years of his leadership. We had the good fortune of knowing him quite well as a friend of our family, and we were very much looking forward to seeing him at the function.

The Principal of the school, Mrs. Talwar was looking her elegant best, and the guests included the elite of the city. After the important dignitaries were seated on the dais, Mrs. Talwar started reading out her welcome speech. Suddenly, the electricity went off. It was not unusual in those days to have a power failure in Delhi, but this was a most unwelcome disruption of the proceedings. We could see that Mrs. Talwar became very worried and frustrated, and was almost in tears. No one could say how long the power breakdown would continue.

We were sitting right in front, and could hear her apologizing in utter desperation to the Air Chief: "Sir, I am extremely sorry for this. But I hope you appreciate, we have no control over this situation."

Air Chief looked absolutely calm.

He smiled and said: "Yes, Madam Principal, we have no control on this situation, but we have full control on how we respond to the situation."

And he added: "No need for you to worry or panic. We can continue with the function in candlelight, while your people work at restoring the power."

The electric power did get restored after a while, and the rest of the function proceeded beautifully. But that response from the Air Chief and his words remained etched in my memory.

How right he was. How often we keep worrying about things over which we have no control. When something does not go the way we expect, we respond with anger or frustration and end up with pain and unhappiness. When someone says something we do not like, we get upset or hurt and end up in bitterness and confrontation. We assume that these negative responses are natural and normal. But we miss the fact that our pain or unhappiness arise from these negative responses.

The situations by themselves do not carry or create pain or unhappiness. At best, they are only triggers for our responses. How we respond to them determines and creates our pain or unhappiness. It is obvious that two persons with different attitudes and orientation would respond differently to the same situation, and their resulting experience of pain or unhappiness would be quite different. Therefore, we should realize that our pain or unhappiness really arise from our own responses. If we control our responses, our pain or unhappiness will also be under our control even if the situation itself is not within our control.

That one remark made by the Air Chief had shown me the way. I realized that I needed to focus upon and control my own response to a situation of conflict – whenever any such situation arises in my day-to-day life. It is by controlling my response, rather than trying to control the situation, that I can avoid getting trapped in the misery and pain. So, my happiness is under my control, whether the relevant situation is within my control or not. I suddenly realized the power of positive thinking, how it can generate the right response, and how it can save me from all the unhappiness. I could see some light now, and it was becoming clear to me what to do.

That evening, when I mentioned this to Raj, he laughed and said: "Aparna, you are thinking too much. It does not work like this in real life. If things go wrong, you are bound to react and get upset. If you do not resist or do not control the situation, it will get out of hand, and everything will go wrong. In our real, practical life, we need action, not philosophy."

"Can you explain to me what you mean?" I asked him.

"It is simple," he said. "If I do not control my people, they will not work. If I do not check my work meticulously, there will be mistakes. You can not take things for granted; you have to work to make them happen. It is true for my work, and it is equally true for yours.

I wanted to explain my understanding of what the Air Chief had said.

I said: "I don't think the Air Chief denied the need to work and the need to do our best in any situation that we face. What I understood him to say was that we need to look at our own response to a situation. It is our response that creates the pain or unhappiness for us. For example, if we stay calm and our response is positive, we can still do whatever the situation demands, but we will not experience pain or unhappiness. In fact, our control on our response will not only avoid these negative feelings, but will enable us to do much better."

"Well, it is very good if you can do that," Raj responded. "Anger, frustration and worry do us no good in any situation. But the million-dollar question is – can we control these when things go wrong or people misbehave? You would have to be a saint to be able to do that. We are ordinary human beings, and it is natural that we get excited or worked-up in such situations. That is how the world works, at least the world that I live and work in."

He smiled, and then asked: "Can you change the world? Good luck, if you can."

I could see that there was no use trying to convince Raj. Instead, I needed to think more about it. It was clear to me that unless there is a fundamental change in the systems in which we live and work, conflicts will continue to arise at various levels. We can not change the systems – at least in the present, and therefore, have no choice but to face the situations of conflict as they arise. The question for me is – how do I respond? If it is true that pain and unhappiness would arise due to my negative response to that situation, the obvious question is – how can I control my response? Does this mean that I have to change my own way of thinking and responding? What do I do to respond positively in a given situation?

I needed to explore this further. I needed to understand what conditions our responses. I needed to know why do we respond the way we do? Then, it occurred to me who can explain this better than the Air Chief himself, who made that profound statement at the Founder's Day function? Why shouldn't I ask him? I decided to wait for an opportunity when I could talk to him.

After two weeks, we were celebrating Varun's 12th birthday. We had invited his school friends and some of our very close family friends. We also invited the Air Chief, as he was close to our family and treated Varun as his grandson. He and his wife accepted our invitation and came for the birthday party. After the party was over, they stayed on for coffee.

The Air Chief was in a relaxed mood, and I took the opportunity of broaching the subject that was on my mind: "Uncle, you gave us valuable guidance the other day when there was power breakdown at Varun's school. Mrs. Talwar was in great distress, and your words comforted her very much."

"There was no reason for her to suffer," he said. "It was not her fault, but she was reacting negatively and making herself miserable."

"You had said that a situation may not be under our control, but our response is within our control. I can now see that our pain and unhappiness arise from our negative response to a situation. But I am not clear how we can control our response to make sure that it does not cause us pain and unhappiness," I asked.

He replied: "Well, the obvious thing to do is to ensure every time that your response is positive, and not negative. Now you will ask me, what is a positive response?"

He looked at me smilingly and then continued: "Ok. I can tell you from my own experience, as I have faced many difficult situations, which have not always been under my control. My prescription for a positive response has been a simple three-step process:

First, I always try to understand and accept the reality of the situation. Second, I take responsibility. Third, I focus on action."

He looked at me, and realized that I wanted to hear more.

He continued in his carefully measured tone: "Listen my child, I am not a philosopher and I do not claim to preach morality or give you a magic formula. All my life I have been a man of action, and I am pretty clear that this approach works in real life. Most of the time, when we face a situation, we refuse to accept it and keep trying to see it the way we had wanted it to be, or the way we have been conditioned by our beliefs and expectations. We do not accept the reality as it is, but we interpret things our way, and mostly our interpretation is colored by our preconceived notions and prejudices. But I take and accept the situation as it is – because that is the only way I can respond to it properly."

"And then I take responsibility for the situation as it is. I see absolutely no point in trying to blame someone else for what has happened. Even if I am not responsible for what may have caused a bad situation and even if it is someone else's fault, the important fact is that the situation is now before me, and I must take responsibility for the situation and handle it."

"This enables me to immediately go to my third step – to focus on action. I have no time to keep talking about it. I must act now as fast as the situation demands. Discussion is helpful so long as it is focused on exploring and deciding on action to be taken, not on finding who is at fault and why. Let somebody else do that. I prefer to focus on the action required to be taken, and I proceed with that as best as possible under the circumstances. I must say, that is how our Air Force works. We have no time to spend on the luxury of talking all the time. We are quite happy to leave that to others."

I said: "Uncle, all of us should then take training in the Air Force. That will save us a lot of unhappiness due to our wrong responses to situations in our lives!"

He smiled and said: "Aparna, it's too late. The Air Force won't take you. You must solve your problems where you are."

I wanted to explore this further.

I asked: "I have one doubt. Let us say, we follow your three-step response process – we accept the reality, take responsibility, and focus on action. It does seem to me that this will most probably save us from the unhappiness that would have been caused by our wrong response. But will that also bring us happiness? I mean, avoiding unhappiness is one thing, and achieving happiness is another thing. Does your approach get us both?"

He laughed, and said: "Aparna, you are really getting smart. Where did you learn all this? I don't think they teach this in your medical colleges. But I really like your question and let me answer it. The first two steps avoid wrong reaction and therefore, save you from unhappiness. It is your third step of action, which brings you happiness. When you take action, you get the result, and the result brings the happiness that you are looking for. Let me also quickly add that these steps are not separate or removed from each other. These are somewhat sequential in the sense that they arise in that order, but are practically simultaneous in the process of responding to a situation."

I did not want to leave the question of happiness.

I persisted with another question: "What if the action is not successful? Then nothing results in happiness."

He was quick to reply: "Yes, of course that is possible. But you are forgetting that you then have a situation where action has not given a successful result. This is the situation before you then, and this is exactly where your response has to be the same three step response. You accept the fact of not being successful, you take responsibility for it, and then focus on new action to be taken in the light of the knowledge and experience you gained in the previous action which was not successful."

He continued: "There is another very important point you should remember. When I ask for action, what I mean is the action, which is under your control. For instance, take a situation, which demands quick action. If that action is under your control, go ahead and take that action. But if that is not within your control, do not waste time on trying to do something, which is outside your power, and do not keep worrying or complaining about it. Instead of wasting your energy on that, you need to focus your attention on changing your own perception, approach and strategy. That would be the right positive response, and will save you from pain and unhappiness even in those situations which are not under your control, either fully or partly."

I really wanted to thank him for clearing up the doubts in my mind.

I smiled and said: "Uncle, this has helped me so much to clear up the confusion in my mind. Now I understand that unhappiness and happiness are two sides of the same coin – both flowing from our response to a given situation before us. Accepting the situation and taking responsibility will save us from unhappiness, and our positive action will bring us the happiness. The three-step process of our response as you have explained is the key for both. Thank you so much."

Interestingly, Raj was more than convinced, and said with a lot of respect: "Uncle, we are really so fortunate to get the benefit of your wisdom and experience. You should come to our home more often."

Air Chief patted him on his back, and his wife hugged me. Varun touched their feet and was rewarded with precious blessings from both of them.

It turned out to be a most memorable birthday party for us.

LATER THAT NIGHT, my mind went back to a situation which had caused a lot of unhappiness in our family. My brother Vipin is three years younger than me. All through his academic career he was a brilliant student and my parents were always very proud of his performance in studies. After graduating from Delhi University, he went to America, did his MBA with major in finance, and then took a job with a top financial services company in New York City. He did quite well and within six years, rose to the position of a Vice President in the company. He married Jennifer, an American girl. This was a love marriage, and although my parents did not quite approve of it, they went along with it. It seemed to all of us that Vipin had settled down in America. Although we missed him, we were happy that he was doing well in life.

Unfortunately, when the global financial crisis hit the world in 2009, his company was forced into a massive restructuring and cost-cutting program. Vipin lost his job. He kept on trying other options, but due to the financial world's continuing crisis, nothing seemed to have worked out for him. My parents tried to persuade him to return to India, but he was not willing to do so, probably because he did not want to face the family for what he saw as his failure both in his career and his personal life. It also seemed to me that Jennifer was never prepared to come to India no matter how much Vipin would have wanted to. Unfortunately, things between them became so bad that Jennifer left and their marriage ended in divorce.

For us in India, this was most shocking. Our cultural background made it very difficult for us to understand Jennifer's action. We could only imagine the traumatic experience of my brother to find his love marriage broken. It left a permanent scar on his psyche and resulted in unhappiness not only for him but for all those who were connected with him. I could also well imagine similar unhappiness that Jennifer must have suffered.

The mere memory of this unfortunate event caused me anguish that night. How much worse was the pain that my brother and his ex-wife were suffering?

My mind was asking – is this not just the case where the response to a situation has caused so much pain and misery? Here was a situation where a man loses his job due to a global financial crisis – something which is outside his control, and the response to that situation leads to a broken marriage – a marriage which was founded upon mutual love. Could that be avoided, if the response was the way the Air Chief had pointed out? Did the couple accept the reality as it existed, did they take the responsibility, and did they focus on action? Both of them were suffering, because they did not respond to the situation positively.

I wish everyone understood this simple and practical idea, and thereby save oneself from the pain and misery being caused by one's own responses to situations outside one's control.

The next day, when I mentioned this to Raj, he not only agreed with me, but said: "I am also seeing things from a different perspective. Now I see that many complicated and long-drawn disputes and litigations persist in our legal field just because the parties are not prepared to accept the reality and take responsibility. Then the action taken by them is almost the reverse of what needs to be done to solve the problem. The result is that there is so much fighting going on and pain and unhappiness continuing for everyone."

"You mean, except for your lawyer fraternity? They all gain out of it, don't they?" I jokingly remarked.

He took it lightly and laughed. "That is unfortunate, and not the way it should be. No good lawyer wants to make money from the pain and unhappiness of others. That is why we have so many alternate dispute resolution processes, like conciliation and arbitration. Although, I am afraid, even those do not work as they should."

After a pause, he added: "You have given me a good idea. I will work on this response theory in some cases which I am already dealing with."

I was happy to hear that, and to see the prospect of the

theory being applied in actual practice. I had the confidence that when Raj took up an idea, he surely made it work.

After a few weeks, he himself told me about his experience.

It was about a litigation, which was going on in the courts for the past 14 years. Originally, the dispute had arisen between two brothers who were running a business in equal partnership. The elder brother had taken the greater part of the responsibility for the business of the firm and the younger brother was dealing with matters relating to accounts, taxation, and finances. In three successive years, the business incurred losses and not only was the firm's capital wiped out but the firm faced substantial loans and liabilities. The younger brother filed a suit against the elder brother holding him responsible for the situation and claiming that he should be fully compensated.

The suit dragged on at various levels in the courts for many years, and during this period, the elder brother died. He must have died a very unhappy person, not only due to the failed business but also due to the action taken against him by his younger brother. After his death, his two sons were substituted in the proceedings, and the case was continuing against the sons, who did not know much about the business, which no longer existed nor about the losses made in it during their father's lifetime. As this was dragging on for years this had completely destroyed the family relationships. Even the second-generation members of the family on both sides were the victims of that situation.

Raj decided to try the three-step response idea and met the younger brother. Raj narrated to me their conversation.

Raj told the younger brother: "I would like you to take a fresh look at the litigation going on with your brother's sons. The situation has changed very much since the case was started."

The brother asked: "Why do you say so? I am still fighting and waiting for the result. What has changed?"

Raj replied: "Everything has changed. Your brother has died. You are now fighting with his sons who had nothing to do with your business, nor the losses made by your brother. Fourteen years have passed since you started the case. I would not be surprised if this goes on for many more years. Don't you think it is time we thought of finding another solution?"

The brother protested: "I can fight till the end. I want to teach them a lesson – to my brother and also his sons."

Raj retorted: "Your brother is no longer in this world. He has gone to heaven. If you want to teach him a lesson, you will have to go and meet him in heaven!"

And then he added: "You will have to wait for that till you die!"

The brother was taken aback to hear this. He kept quiet, and then asked: "What do you want me to do?"

Raj told him in a helpful tone: "Listen to me. I am your lawyer, and I will always look after your interest. This litigation is not taking you anywhere, and you must accept the reality of this situation, as it exists now. Your brother has died, 14 years have gone by, you have got nothing so far, and your fight can drag on for many more years. This is the reality of the situation at present. Unless you realize and accept it, nothing can be done to solve the problem."

The brother seemed to understand, and said: "I am not responsible for this. What can I do? Whatever is the situation, it is not in my control."

Raj said: "You are right. You are not responsible for this situation. But you do have the responsibility of finding a solution. Otherwise, you will not get anything, and everyone will continue to suffer because of this on-going fight – including your family and your brother's family."

And then Raj softly added: "Please also remember that you are now the eldest member of both the families. You also have a responsibility for that reason."

The brother thought for a while, and then said: "OK. Let me say that I see the reality of the situation now which is very different from what it was when I filed the case against my brother. Let me say, I also take whatever responsibility you are trying to explain to me. But what can I do? The case is before the court. You have to handle it and win it for me. What is there for me to do?"

Raj took the opportunity of explaining to him the need for a positive action, and said: "Yes, I will of course do that if you insist. But there is a much better course of action you can take. You can settle the whole thing by arbitration. I can seek the permission of the court to do that, and then the matter can be resolved quite quickly. You can stop fighting, and that will stop all the pain and unhappiness being caused to both the families."

Raj told me that the younger brother realized the reality of the changed situation, his own responsibility, and the need to focus on positive action. This became possible because Raj was able to explain to him the logic and wisdom of adopting this three step response. For the first time, the brother was made to realize the reality of the situation as it existed, both as it was when the suit was filed, and also in the changed circumstances after the death of his elder brother. Raj also made him aware of his own responsibility for the losses incurred in the business, and also for finding a solution. The younger brother then saw the need for a different response and a different action on his part.

Raj found a respected retired judge to conduct the arbitration, and the entire matter was successfully resolved. To me it seemed to be a happy ending for a very unhappy situation, thanks to the three-step response.

In my own medical practice, I also started seeing opportunities of adopting this idea of three-step response in situations, which often seemed difficult.

A very interesting example of such a situation appeared before me in the case of a woman in her mid-thirties who was admitted to my hospital for a delivery. This was going to be her third child, and the two previous ones were daughters. She was very concerned that this third child should be a son. She wanted to be assured about that but as per the ethics of my profession, I refused to carry out any test for that purpose. Finally, the child was delivered in my hospital, and as it turned out, this was a girl.

I always expected the parents to rejoice on a safe and successful delivery and the arrival of a new baby in the family. But in this case, it was creating too much unhappiness for the woman, and she was totally distraught. Her husband and her mother-in-law were not only greatly upset, but were very angry with this woman for her failure to give birth to a son, and were in fact blaming her for it. I was totally unable to understand this reaction, until I found out that the mother-in-law had threatened her daughter-in-law and prevailed upon her son to divorce the woman, or take another wife. I was literally shocked when I was told that according to the custom and code applicable to them, it was possible to give an instant divorce, and also to have a second wife. It was so clear to me that this response was going to cause unimaginable misery and pain to the woman for a situation which arose for no fault of hers, and which was totally outside her control.

I thought that I should try the three-step response idea.

When the husband of the woman came to the hospital, I asked him to stay back to talk to me separately. He was at least prepared to listen to me and I talked to him on a one-to-one basis.

I initiated the conversation: "You are now a proud father of a lovely baby girl, with her two sisters in your home. How do you plan to celebrate this occasion? I hope you will invite me for that."

He was not prepared for this. He just said: "Doctor, you must be joking. My mother and I are greatly disappointed, not happy. We very much wanted a son, not another daughter. What is there to celebrate?"

I replied: "Yes, it is nice to have a son in the family. But daughters are equally welcome. They bring so much happiness. Look at me. I am also someone's daughter. Do you know how happy my parents are to have me as their daughter?"

He softened a bit, and said: "Doctor, you and your family are different. My mother wants a grand-son, not a grand-daughter. This is the third time my wife has let us down. I do not know what will happen now."

I well understood that he was hinting at a possible divorce or a second wife for himself. I wanted to shake him up into a realization of the reality of the situation and his own responsibility.

I spoke to him in a very firm tone, and said: "You are blaming your wife. I am a medical doctor and I must tell you that you are equally responsible for the conception right from the beginning. Let me also tell you that when the conception takes place, the baby's gender is determined by the chromosome coming from the father. Therefore, please do not blame your wife, and please do not mislead yourself in doing so. You can not run away from your responsibility."

He was upset to hear this, and kept quiet. I then continued in an equally firm voice: "I can see your problem. You just built up an image of a son when your wife conceived. Maybe you built up images of sons when you married the woman. But all that was your own mental image that you made. It was not the reality then, and it is not the reality now. The reality is that you have three daughters now, and you are as much responsible for that situation as your wife is. Am I right or wrong?"

I then firmly told him: "Please understand that both the parents are responsible for the child – whether it is a boy or a girl. You must accept your responsibility and stop blaming your wife."

He remained quiet, and kept looking at me.

Nobody had talked to him like I did. After I spoke to him, he was able to see the situation in a new perspective and not in his preconceived image; and I think for the first time he was willing to accept the reality of the situation as it then existed. I had to be somewhat abrasive in making him aware of his 'responsibility'. As for the need for action to handle the situation, it was proper to do something to satisfy him and his mother, and at the same time save his wife from pain and unhappiness.

I wanted to help, and said in a soft tone: "I fully share your keen desire to have a son in the family. I also respect the feelings of your mother. We can do something for that. I can arrange for you to adopt a newborn baby boy. Why don't you talk to your mother and your wife and let me know? I will be happy to do that for you."

He was able to see the merit of this positive action, and looked quite relieved from the tension he was carrying when he came to me.

To my great relief, his mother, he and his wife accepted this suggestion. We did just that.

After a few days both the husband and wife came together to see me. I was happy to see that they brought with them both the new babies – the boy and the girl. I examined them and found everything fine.

When they were ready to leave, the woman had tears in her eyes. She did not speak a word. She just handed over a small package to me, folded her hands and put her palms together to show her gratitude. I opened the package and found a nice Sari that she had brought for me as a gift. Normally, I would never accept a gift from my patients. But I could not refuse this one. This meant so much to me as a token of her genuine feelings.

I was deeply moved, but held back the tears of happiness in my eyes.

I continue to believe to this day, that everyone in that family has remained happy – the woman, her husband, and her mother-in-law. I had such a good feeling that all the pain, misery and unhappiness were avoided for all of them, thanks again to the three step response.

In my practice as a child specialist, I was dealing with children and their parents on a regular basis. I started seeing opportunities for explaining to the parents the three step response process, and how it affected the child and the happiness of everyone in the family. In so many cases, the performance of the child in school did not come up to the standard adopted by the mother or father on the basis of a pre-conceived image in their minds. Many a times, such an image was unconsciously picked up by them from other parents and became a part of their own ego, which was then being imposed upon their child. This was far from the reality, and almost always failed to realistically understand and integrate the qualities and capacities of their child.

Once I started looking, I could see so many instances. The most common example, which recurred from case to case, was the choice of educational program and future career, and the standards of desired performance imposed upon the child by the parents. Due to such imposition, the child often went into depression or indifference. The performance deteriorated, and that made the situation even worse. Instead of seeing the reality and taking responsibility, the parents either pleaded ignorance or blamed the child. It was so common to see a mother shouting and rebuking her child, although she was doing that with the best of intention on her part, yet under a mistaken belief that she was doing it for the good of the child. Whenever I was able to explain to them and make them see the reality and accept the responsibility for their response, there was a dramatic change in the performance of the child.

I am reminded of an interesting case of Deepak who was a classmate of my son Varun. Deepak's father was an engineer working in a very senior position in a multinational company, and he had decided that the best career for his only son Deepak was to become an engineer like his father. But Deepak hated mathematics and loved music. He wanted to take music as one of the subjects in school, but that was not allowed as the parents thought otherwise. Deepak's class test and examination results were very disappointing, not only in the subject of mathematics, but also in other subjects.

Deepak often came to our home to meet his good friend

Varun, and on one occasion, Varun told me about Deepak's problem. I could see that his parents had failed to appreciate and accept the reality of Deepak's aptitude and capability. They were also ignoring their responsibility to take ownership of the situation and were instead placing the responsibility upon Deepak for his poor performance at school.

Varun pleaded with me to speak to Deepak's parents. I did not know them well, yet I arranged to meet them one evening at Panchsheel Club where I am a member. This is a very nice club in south Delhi. I also asked Varun and Deepak to join us. At the last moment, Raj also was able to join us.

The weather turned out to be very pleasant and we decided to have our tea and snacks in the garden. I did not quite know how to start the conversation about Deepak's problem. Raj came to my rescue.

He asked Deepak: "Do you know that your friend Varun has been telling us that you sing very well? We have never heard you sing. When are you going to do that for us?"

Deepak kept quiet.

His father Mr. Mathur spoke: "Yes, he likes to sing. But he must learn from his friend Varun how to do well in his studies. Unless he does well in his studies, singing will not make him a good engineer."

Varun looked at Deepak, and very innocently tried to explain: "But uncle, Deepak does not want to be an engineer. I know he loves music. One day he can be a great person in the world of music."

Then he turned to Deepak and asked: "Am I right, Deepak?"

Deepak looked rather scared and just nodded in agreement.

I took the opportunity, and said: "Mr. Mathur, I know it is none of my business to interfere in this. But Varun and Deepak are close friends and love each other. As Varun's mother, I treat Deepak as my own child. I am told he is not doing well in his studies. It seems to me he is losing interest. Is it possible that he can also do what is his real passion? Can he be allowed to take music as one of his subjects at school?"

Mr. Mathur was quite explicit about his thoughts, and said: "Aparna Ji, I really appreciate your concern for Deepak. But I am equally clear that he can follow his passion for music later in his life. Right now, he must devote all his attention to his studies and become a good engineer. That is the best thing for him to do."

Then he added: "Aparna Ji, you are a doctor and specialize in child psychology. So you can very well understand how important it is for parents to guide their children towards a right career."

Hearing him, I decided to deal with this issue in a straight forward manner, and said:

"Yes Mr. Mathur, parents must guide. But the choice of career has to be on the basis of the aptitude and interest of the child, not what the parents have decided in their minds as a preconceived idea. And let me also say, no career is bad. What matters is how well it is pursued and accomplished."

I then added: "Can you say that sport is a bad career? If a child has the passion and promise, he can excel in sports. Look at cricket. If Sachin Tendulkar's parents had insisted that their son must become a doctor or a lawyer, he could not have achieved the greatest success in his life as the best batsman in the world. Similarly, if Mahender Singh Dhoni's parents had not allowed him to pursue his passion for cricket, we would have missed the best captain of the Indian cricket team in recent times. His team has now won the World Cup after defeating the teams from Australia, Sri Lanka and Pakistan. This is a historic achievement, which becomes possible when young people are able to pursue their passion in life. Who knows, whether Deepak with all his talent in music, would one day achieve the same glorious height as achieved by Shri Ravi Shankar or Birju Maharaj in the filed of music."

Mrs. Mathur was most receptive to my words.

She said: "Aparna, we also want Deepak to achieve great success in life. As a good doctor, what would you advise us to do? We only want the best for him."

I was very happy to hear this.

I said: "Every parent wants that for their child. But each child is different. The first thing we have to do is to leave aside our own preconceived ideas, and try to understand the reality of the situation of the child. As I see it, the reality of Deepak's situation is that he has great potential as well as passion for a career in music – not in engineering. If we recognize this reality, there is good reason to let him explore the subject of music along with his other subjects in school. His performance itself will then show what is good for him and what is not."

Mrs. Mathur, seemed to understand, and said: "Ok. Good that you have explained this to us so nicely. We will think about it."

Once I saw that they were prepared to see the reality of their child's situation, I did not want to leave it at this uncertain and ambiguous state of their thinking.

I said: "That is very good. But you have to take responsibility for this situation. It is no use being disappointed or finding fault with Deepak's results in school. You must take responsibility, and choose the right action. If you ask me, the right action is to be flexible in choosing the subjects at this stage. Just let him have music as a subject of his choice along with the other subjects in his study program."

Mr. Mathur was listening to me quite attentively.

He patted Deepak on his back, and said in a very affectionate manner: "Deepak, your Aunty has convinced me. You may go ahead with your music. But you must promise me very good results now."

I had never seen Varun so happy and Deepak smiling so brightly. We had a most pleasant evening over tea and rather sumptuous snacks. Both Varun and Deepak happily helped themselves to big helpings of ice creams!

Deepak took music as one of the main subjects in his study program in school. It was amazing to see the transformation in him. He not only secured the highest marks in music theory and practical tests regularly thereafter, but was also able to improve his overall performance in other subjects. Obviously, he had found what he wanted to do, and was motivated to do that best. His parents had accepted the reality of their son's interests, strengths and weaknesses. They took the responsibility, and made it possible for the right action to follow. Their three-step response turned the situation into a success story for the boy and avoided the unhappiness that was arising from their earlier negative response to the same situation.

THE THREE STEP APPROACH for our responses seemed quite useful for dealing with a variety of situations in our lives. I wanted to explore this further and also to share it with others.

An opportunity to do so came up after a few weeks. Lions Club in Delhi used to organize an annual function to celebrate its Charter Night. As part of the full day program, they usually invited a guest speaker to deliver a talk on a subject of general interest. This year they invited me to speak on a subject of my choice. I decided to speak on the issue of 'our responses to adverse situations and their role in our happiness'.

I could not have asked for a better audience. The members of the club and their guests came from all walks of life, were educated and obviously, were successful in their business or vocation. They listened with full attention, and I think, well understood the three-step response, that is, accepting the reality of a situation, taking responsibility, and focusing on action. The question-and-answer session at the end of my talk evoked a lot of interest. In fact, I found some of the questions quite helpful in further clarifying my own understanding. I still remember some of the questions and answers.

One member asked: "If you say, the first step is to accept the situation, does it mean that we do not question it at all, even if it is a wrong situation? Does that mean that we just live with it, even if it is not correct?"

I replied: "No, that is not what the approach requires you to do. I did not ask you to accept the situation. I only asked you to accept the 'reality' of the situation. We have a tendency to look at a situation not as it really is but as we think it to be. Our perception is colored by our own notions and expectations. This means that instead of knowing the reality and taking appropriate action accordingly, we end up with inappropriate action."

I then added: "Let me give you an example. Many of you are in the world of business. If you face a situation where you have incurred a loss on a particular contract, isn't that a reality, which needs to be accepted first? It is a fact that there is a loss and that is something, which has already happened. If you are not willing to accept that reality, you will not be able to find the cause and take the required action. On the contrary, if the reality is disregarded, you may be spending your time and energy on questioning the factual position of loss, or blaming others within your own organization, or blaming the entire system, or trying to justify it by some reason or other. This is what happens in most situations of a failure – whether a business is making a loss, or a child is not performing well in school, or someone in the family is not behaving according to your expectations. Therefore, as a first step, you must find out and accept the reality of the situation as it exists."

I further explained: "Once you see and accept the reality, you need to take responsibility – both as regards the situation as well as the necessity for taking action in that situation. Please also remember the third step in the response process – that is, to focus on action. As I explained in my talk, this needs to be a positive action, and this means that you have to focus on action which is under your control instead of persisting with the effort to do something which is not under your control."

Another member questioned: "Why do you say that we do not see the reality of situation? When something goes wrong, we know what has happened."

I had to point out: "It is not that simple. Usually, there is a difference between what an incident actually is, and what is our perception and interpretation of that incident. What we interpret is colored by our pre-existing ideas, beliefs, and memory of our past experiences. These get set in our minds, and when we look at an incident, our understanding is conditioned by these. For example, if you have developed a negative opinion about someone – whether that person is within your family or in you social or business circle – you will see the action or behavior of that person in a negative perspective, even if it is actually with good intention. This is a very common problem in our relationships. Once we get an image set in our minds, we just continue to live with that and see everything in that light."

I continued: "Our own ego can be another major problem. If you have built up your ego, as most of us do, on the basis of your own beliefs or images about yourself, this can color your vision without your even realizing it. But let me add that I am not asking you to give up all these ideas, beliefs or experiences. I am asking you just to become aware of these consciously, so that when you look at a situation and try to understand its reality, you have a clear view, uncluttered by all these notions and influences. Just remove your colored glasses first and then you can see the reality of the situation."

Another young person asked: "When someone has misbehaved or has done something wrong, what responsibility can we take for his behavior or wrong doing?"

I replied: "No, I am not asking you to take responsibility for him, nor for his behavior or action. I am only asking you to take responsibility for your own response to that situation.

The real question here is how you respond to that situation. Whether you suffer or avoid unhappiness will depend upon your response. So, when I say you take responsibility, I mean that you take responsibility for your own response."

Then, I added: "Someone rightly said – 'responsibility' means 'response + ability', that is, your ability to respond. I suggest, you should remember this meaning of the word 'responsibility'."

Another member asked: "Can you explain how we can focus on action?"

"Yes, I am happy you have asked this question. This is a very important step in your response process. In fact, the first two steps of acceptance and responsibility are to enable the third step of action. By 'action', I mean a positive action. For instance, complaining about a situation is also an action, but it has no positive value. Similarly, action focusing on things, which are not in your control, would result only in wasted energy and time. Focus on action means a pragmatic approach. This requires realistic and positive thinking. I am sure all of you have got that ability; it is just a question of your becoming aware of the need to use that ability in a given situation."

More questions were asked about the action to be taken in a given situation and many examples were discussed. Basically, these revolved around finding a way for settling the differences or disputes instead of putting up a fight in every case.

Then, a very interesting question was asked by a young man: "When you talk of action, do you believe in taking selfless action? We are told that our highest scriptures like the Bhagvad Gita lay down the principle that action should be selfless and without any expectation of reward or result. I am sure you would have heard the saying – 'work is thy duty, reward not thy concern'. Do you agree with this, and do you think we can really follow this?"

This was a very important issue, and I did not wish to miss the opportunity to clarify this aspect of action.

I replied: "You must give me time to explain as this is a very important point. Let me tell you, this is a wrong interpretation of what our ancient scriptures have said. In fact, I have not found this in any of the scriptures that I know of, including the Gita. This interpretation comes from the commentaries written by various scholars, and it is necessary that the confusion created by these commentaries must be cleared. Let me make just three points to clear this up."

I continued and said: "First: The particular shloka in the Gita which says *"Karmanye va adhikaraste, ma phalesh kadachen"* literally means that your action is under your control, not the result of the action. This is true in real life. You can execute and control your action, but once you have done that, the result follows from that action and not from your control over the result. This shloka emphasizes the cause-and-effect relationship between action and result. It is not correct to interpret this to say that you should give up the result or the benefit flowing from your action."

I wanted to explain it further and continued: "You may have heard about the word 'detachment'. This is often interpreted as meaning that we should perform the action but detach ourselves from the result. Now, detachment does not mean renunciation or giving up. Being detached does not mean that you renounce or give up the reward or the benefit from the action. It only means that while performing the action, you should keep yourself mentally detached from the result. This means that your entire focus should then remain on the action, and you should not think or worry about the reward from that action or your success or failure. Only then will you be able to fully concentrate and perform the action in the best possible manner."

They were listening attentively..

So, I continued: "Second: "The same Gita clearly tells us in another shloka,

> *"Yogasthah kur karman, sangam tyakte Dhananjaye,*
> *asidhyo samo bhutva, samatvam yogamuchyate."*

Literally, this means: "Be established in yoga and then dedicate yourself to action – free from attachment and maintaining your equanimity whether in success or in failure. O Arjuna, that state of equilibrium is called yoga."

I paused, and then added: "My dear friends, this is the essence of the principle of action enunciated in the Gita. Please note that this shloka defines yoga as 'equilibrium' – a state of equanimity both in success and failure. It directs you to engage in action by first establishing yourself in that state of equilibrium. When you take an action while you are in a state of equilibrium that is a perfect way to take action and get the best result. This does not say nor even remotely suggest that you should give up the result. It only asks you to maintain your equilibrium both in success and failure, so that your action achieves the best result."

I added: "In fact, in another shloka, the Gita clearly states: "Yoga karmasu kaushalam" which literally means that "Yoga is excellence in action." So, the Gita asks you for excellence in action, and tells you how to achieve that by engaging in action while remaining in a state of equilibrium both in success and failure. Any interpretation of Gita that it asks you to give up the result of your action is not correct."

I pointed out: "This is the action that you need to take as the third step in your response to a situation, as we discussed earlier."

The young man who had asked the question seemed to understand what I was saying, but asked: "Can you give me an example of how this is possible in real life?"

I quickly responded, and asked him if he played tennis? "Yes," he nodded.

Then, I said: "When you play tennis, you play to win, not to lose. But it is natural that you may win one round and you may lose the other. If in the final result you win, you get the winner's trophy or whatever the reward is. But while you are playing the game, your total focus must remain on the ball and on your action to play the ball with the best shot. In that moment, you are mentally detached from the trophy or the reward. You want to play the best game; and you do that irrespective of the result of winning or losing during each stage of the game, or at the end. In fact, if you keep thinking of the trophy or reward, you would lose your concentration on your action to play the ball. You would then probably lose the game. But if you remain mentally detached from the end result, you can play the game well and bring excellence into your action."

Looking at him, I added: "My dear friend, in this sense, your life is also comparable to a game – a game that you must play in the best possible manner. That becomes possible when your entire focus is on your action, and when you are able to detach yourself from the result – whether it is success or failure."

Rather unexpectedly, the audience clapped to show their approval of this example.

I thought they were quite happy to listen to my long-drawn talk, and my impression was confirmed by the last comment made by a young lady in the audience.

She stood up and said: "It is so good to know that our happiness or unhappiness comes from our own response to a situation, and not from the situation itself. So, when we have our responses under our control, we also have our happiness or unhappiness under our control. To me, this means that we take responsibility for our own happiness, instead of depending upon others. That is great. Your three step response has really helped me to understand this. I think, now I know what to do."

I smiled and concluded my talk.

"Yes, we know what to do… Let's do that."

CHAPTER 4

How to be?

I HAD ANOTHER VERY BUSY day at the hospital. I had to handle two complicated delivery cases, both requiring surgery. My colleague, another gynecologist was on leave that day and I had to take in her patients as well. When I returned home at about 7pm that evening, I only had energy to take a shower and get into bed.

I was surprised to see Raj had also come home. Due to his evening briefing sessions in his chamber, he would normally come home around 9pm or even later. When I asked him if he was feeling alright, he said: "Have you forgotten? We have to go to Malhotras' son's wedding reception today."

I then remembered that their son was married the previous week. Since we could not attend the wedding, we had decided to go to the reception to convey our good wishes to the couple. I was really tired and asked Raj to go alone, but he insisted that I must accompany him, and promised that we would not stay there for long.

Wedding receptions are occasions where women do not miss the opportunity to show off their best dresses and jewellery. Much against my wishes, I too had to dress appropriately for the occasion.

I asked: "Raj, what should I wear for the reception? I think I need to wear a nice sari. Can you select one for me?"

Without even looking at me, he said: "Just put on whatever you are comfortable with. Don't worry too much about your dress."

I got quite annoyed, and shot back: "Of course, I will. But you are so indifferent. You don't care how your wife looks at a large function."

He was obviously taken aback. He came to me, and said: "That is not true. I care, and I care very much. I just don't want you to take unnecessary strain for these things."

"Yes, I understand. How I look is not important for you at all. So why should you care about my dress or what I wear for the party?" I did not conceal my annoyance.

He held my hand, and said in a rather mischievous way: "Aparna, your dress is of no importance, because you are so beautiful and you look so charming and graceful in whatever dress you wear."

I gave him a stern look, but he kept smiling, and added: "Why should you blame me if I look at you and not at your dress, and I can't take my eyes off you? I think everyone else at the reception will probably do the same!"

I could not help laughing at his clever words. I smiled and said: "You are so good at the art of flattery. I do not know how to handle that. All lawyers seem to survive on that, and always make a fool of us."

He kept smiling and said nothing.

I then shot back: "In my next life, I will never take a lawyer for my husband! Ok, let me get ready now."

I had forgotten my fatigue, and actually felt much better after this cross-fire dialogue with Raj. As I dressed up, I felt amused and relaxed, and quietly liked the subtle humor that was typical of Raj.

A little later, as we entered the beautifully decorated reception hall, Mrs. Malhotra gave us a warm welcome, and said to me: "I am so happy you and Raj have come. Aparna, you look so good. You look really great. Thank you for coming."

She took us to the new bride and introduced us. The social etiquette being over, we left after a while. As Raj was driving back, he asked me if I was feeling better. Yes, I said.

Suddenly, I asked him: "Did you hear Mrs. Malhotra saying that I was looking so good? You know how tired and run down I am feeling inside, but she says I am looking good outside. So, that is all that matters – how I look outside. No one knows or cares how I feel inside me."

Raj looked a little taken aback. He said that he cared very much how I was feeling, and even regretted that he had forced me to go to the reception.

We took a light meal at our home, and then went early to bed. The next morning at breakfast, he mentioned that he was not happy at my discomfort on my perception about how I felt inside and how I looked outside. He even said that this showed some kind of dichotomy in my perception about myself which can keep causing unnecessary stress, and I should not think too much about these things. We left the subject at that.

That evening, Raj told me about one Mr. Pawan Ji, whom he knew personally. He suggested that I meet him and take some rejuvenating treatments at his spa and healthcare center. Pawan Ji was working in this spa and healthcare center in the city where the elite of the town and celebrities from all over were coming to regularly. Pawan Ji was an astro-physicist and had become famous for his knowledge in energy-based medicines and treatments. He had qualified as a software engineer from one of the prestigious Indian Institutes of Technology, but later switched over to his chosen field – a combination of astro-science, ayurveda, and energy medicine.

He was quite successful in his diagnostic analysis of the persons coming to the healthcare center. He would take a reading of their energy fields and combine it with clinical observations and conventional pathological tests. His spa followed a holistic approach. This required that apart from analyzing the physical state of the person, it was necessary to understand the state of underlying energy fields in the body and mind and any imbalances or inadequacies at those levels. Based upon such analysis, he worked out for each person a protocol which combined energy-based and herbal treatments, yoga, and meditation techniques. Overall, he adopted an integrated approach to the treatment of body, mind and spirit. This was one of the main reasons for his popularity and the success of the spa and healthcare center.

Raj suggested that he would get an appointment with Pawan Ji whenever I wanted to see him. I took his phone number and promised to talk to him myself.

When I phoned Pawan Ji the next day, he talked to me very nicely. In the course of our conversation, when I told him what I was interested in, he mentioned that he held a workshop once every month. He invited me to attend the next workshop where I could go into the subject in greater detail and also have the benefit of interaction with other participants. The subject for the next workshop was 'Our perceptions and beliefs'. This was coming up on the following Saturday. It was a full-day program, and the maximum number was limited to 12 persons so as to allow better attention and interaction for every participant. I checked my schedule and found that I could attend this, and so I did.

The workshop was held in the conference room at the healthcare center. After introducing himself, Pawan Ji asked the participants to give a self-introduction and to tell what they expected from the workshop. There were 12 participants and all of them were well educated. Out of these, one was teaching psychology at a college, two were working in a software company, four or five held executive positions in some large business houses, and one lady was a housewife and social worker. I was the only one from the medical field.

Pawan Ji had a soft voice and smiling face, and radiated a feeling of peace. Although none of us knew him earlier, we felt quite comfortable in his presence. He had listened carefully when the participants spoke about what they were looking for.

He spoke slowly, choosing his words carefully: "All our life, without realizing, each one of us continues to live on two levels – one in the outside world around us, and the other within our inner self. We may call these levels 'Outer-me' and 'Inner-me'. This does not mean that we become two persons instead of one. The Outer-me and Inner-me may be better understood as two personalities or two faces of the same person, or two sides of the same coin, but the two are very different from each other for several reasons."

"The Outer-me is conditioned by the external environment around us, our social norms and beliefs, and the cultural background of the society in which we live. Our education and training seek to develop our Outer-me to meet the challenge of being successful in life as per the accepted parameters of society. Such success involves active engagement in the battle of life, meeting the demands of family, relatives and friends, and carrying a burden of many other obligations assumed by us – either by choice or by force of circumstances."

He continued: "This becomes a never-ending process, and a major part of our energy and effort continues to be spent on this. The reward or the justification for all this is supposed to be found in the happiness that this is expected to give us in many ways – for example, by a sense of achievement of success in the world, by the power or prestige we are able to acquire and exercise, by a satisfaction of having done our duty as a member of the society, or by the fulfillment of our own emotions arising from our relationships and thoughts. The Outer-me holds on to this pattern as much as possible, and requires great effort and energy for doing that."

"In order to achieve ever-greater success in the world, the Outer-me "becomes increasingly aggressive and dominating, and the Inner-me becomes quiet and suppressed. As the Outer-me pushes on in the external world, the Inner-me keeps silently watching this constant and never-ending process."

"As time passes, this process continues unabated, but our energy and resources undergo a change either with age or due to other changes in our conditions. This then results in increasing effort, strain and stress for us. The expected happiness becomes more elusive and difficult to achieve; yet by force of habit or lack of choice, and despite the increasing effort and strain, the Outer-me pushes the process on."

"Ever so often, during some moments of peace and quiet, we become aware of the other side of the coin – our Inner-me. Whenever we are able to step back from our Outer-me and become aware of our Inner-me, we look at things from a very different perspective. We become aware of the fact that the process going on at the level of the Outer-me is a never-ending process, that the happiness supposed to be achieved by it is very short-lived, fleeting and elusive, and at the end of it all, it is turning out to be a losing battle."

"As we look back at our own past life lived at the level of Outer-me, we become aware of the numerous phases and variety of experiences which came into our life but did not last, many relationships which slipped away, many achievements for which we worked so hard but at some point of time lost interest, and many pleasures and pains in our life which we went through for reasons still not clear."

Pawan Ji paused for a while to let us absorb the impact of what he had said about the Outer-me. He then turned his attention to the Inner-me.

He said: "When we become aware of the Inner-me, we become quiet, just like the nature of Inner-me. We then become aware of many questions, which were always there, but were pushed back and forgotten. We wonder about the true identity of our own self, the purpose of all that is going on in our lives, and the meaning of our own existence. Our life lived so far seems so incomplete and inadequate, and at the level of Inner-me we feel so lonely. Many relationships at the level of Outer-me extending to our family, relatives and friends, suddenly look artificial and incapable of connecting with our Inner-me."

Pawan Ji looked at us, and slowly said in a sober tone: "In our workshop today, we will try to understand our Outer-me and Inner-me and address some of these questions."

Everyone was listening with rapt attention.

Pawan Ji then added: "When each one of you was telling me what you expected from this workshop, I could see that you all have similar questions. Let me first ask: Are you aware of your Outer-me and Inner-me, and if so, which one of the two would you choose to nourish and follow?"

There was pin-drop silence.

After a pause, the housewife said: "I never looked at it that way. But after listening to you, I can say that I am now aware of two faces of myself – one for the outside world, and the other inside me. But I do not know which one to follow."

Taking a cue from that comment, the teacher asked: "But why can't we make them one, or at least reconcile the two?"

Pawan Ji looked around and asked: "Would anyone like to comment on that?"

I took the initiative, and said: "It seems to me that our Outer-me is basically our 'ego' which is projected as our face in the external world. It is our ego that makes our Outer-me different from our Inner-me. I think you all know what I mean by ego."

Pawan Ji encouraged me to explain, and I continued: "As I understand it, we build up an image about ourselves, which is what we think we are. This image of ours is not what we really are, but it is what we would like to be seen as by others around us. This perceived image is our ego. The process of building up our ego starts very early in life and continues through our education and work. By the time we reach a certain level of maturity, our ego expands and includes a wide range of our notions, such as our strengths and qualities, our power and prestige, and our perceived positions within our family, workplace and society. Over the years, as we grow we start believing that image is our identity – that is what we are. We assume that image to be the reality and forget that we are the one who constructed it over the years."

I noticed Pawan Ji's gentle appreciative nod and smile, which indicated that he had liked my explanation.

He took over from me, and said: "This is a very good description of the Outer-me. As you can now see, this is based upon our own ego. You can also see that our ego is like layers upon layers of perceptions and beliefs, which are acquired and added as we move on in life. This is what makes the Outer-me different from the Inner-me. It also follows that if the ego is built upon our own notions and perceptions, the reality can be very different. And if that is so, this can cause quite a few problems."

He then posed a question: "Let me ask, how many of you think that your image and identity in the external world are important and must be projected in the best possible way?"

Everyone was in agreement, and the young man who was a business executive responded: "Of course, that is important both in our personal life as well as in the outside business world. A major factor in our success is how well we position ourselves in the outside world and how well we build our image. And as I said, this is equally true in our personal life. But, Pawan Ji, what is your point?"

Pawan Ji replied: "My point is simple. All we need to do is to remember that although our image and identity in the external world are relevant for our Outer-me, but the fact remains that these have been constructed by us for that purpose. We must not forget that these are projections of our own ego at our personal level, and therefore, these should not mislead us to believe that they define or represent our real self or our Inner-me. If we do not remember this very important fact, we will make the mistake of viewing our circumstances and relationships within the perspective and background of our ego. This is like viewing the situations in our life through colored glasses or a colored filter of our ego. This will give us a distorted view and make our responses inappropriate. Please remember that it is our wrong response to a situation that causes unhappiness and pain for us; and all that can be avoided if our responses are protected from our own ego."

The young man then asked: "Are you saying we need to drop our ego?"

Pawan Ji was quick to reply: "It would be wonderful if you could do that; and it would solve most of your problems! As you can see, conflicts arise and persist in all walks of life due to clash of egos. Mostly, egos are only images and have little or no basis in reality, but people fight for their egos and suffer so much unhappiness and misery due to their inability to differentiate their notions of ego from the reality."

Then he added: "I do realize that people will not give up their ego. Their Outer-me will not allow that. But it is good enough if they can remain fully aware of their own ego. If they are fully aware of their ego, they can judge whether a particular situation is arising due to their ego or it is based upon reality. Ego is like a trap in which you can fall if you are not careful. So, it is good to be aware of your ego; and that awareness itself will save you from giving wrong responses to the situations arising before you. Why should you suffer and become unhappy because of your own ego? Why can't you act in a more sensible way?"

I was reminded of the cause-and-effect relationship between one's response to a situation and the consequent unhappiness, as explained to me by Air Chief Marshall OP Mehra when I had met him at my son's birthday party. I had understood that a wrong response from me would result in my unhappiness; but I still did not know what causes me to give a wrong response, and how it can be avoided? After listening to Pawan Ji, I realized that it is our ego that causes a wrong response; and our awareness of our own ego can enable us to avoid that mistake.

We all took a half-an-hour break for a light lunch.

When we reassembled, Pawan Ji continued: "We have discussed what ego is, how it shapes our Outer-me and how it affects our responses to a situation arising before us. Let me now explain to you two other important factors which condition our Outer-me, and hence, how these also affect the way we live and interact with others. These are: Fear and the Belief System."

"Let me deal first with fear. If you take a closer look at your own life, you will find so much fear, both at your conscious and sub-conscious levels."

"The interesting paradox is that most of the time we do not even realize that fear has taken hold of our mind, our attitude, our thinking, and our responses. We are not even aware that many of our actions are being conditioned by a fear complex within us. We may call it by any other name – for example, a personal sense of insecurity, uncertainty about events, or just plain anxiety or lurking doubt about what may happen in future. By whatever name these may be called, they are manifestation of the same basic phenomenon of fear which has entered our minds."

He continued: "A moment's introspection will show you that fear has overshadowed your mind in reference to almost everything – known or unknown. You may have fear of the known, and also fear of the unknown. For instance, everyone knows that death is certain. Therefore, the fear of death is a fear of the known. On the other hand, while death as an event is known, the timing of death remains unknown, and this uncertainty causes fear of the unknown. Even when we do not explicitly recognize the fear of the unknown, it causes anxiety and fear at our sub-conscious level."

Pawan Ji then proceeded to elaborate how to deal with fear: 'Our responses to deal with the fear of the known, and our responses to deal with the fear of the unknown, are not necessarily the same. The known situations mostly relate to the external world and the outer circumstances within which we live. For instance, fear of the known may arise from financial insecurity which can relate to various economic issues like losing a job or failing in business or profession. Similarly, fear of the known may arise from insecurity about one's place in society and status within the system – such as the worry about not being accepted at the level of one's immediate family or in the larger dimension of the society. Another source of fear could be the uncertainty about our own capacity to deal with and adapt to changes happening around us – such as changes in our personal relationships, or our work, or our place of work and residence. Or one may just have a lurking fear about one's own physical safety and survival as one moves around in the world."

Explaining this issue further, Pawan Ji said: "Fear of the known is usually addressed by known responses. For instance, one may take recourse to accumulation of wealth for mitigating the fear of financial insecurity, or acquisition of social status or political power in order to mitigate the fear of losing one's place or position in society, or acquisition of weapons or safety devices to mitigate the risk of physical damage to oneself."

He continued: "Unlike the fear of the known, the fear of the unknown may not be capable of being clearly identified and provided for. Fear of the unknown tends to be more difficult to deal with. One may never feel certain or satisfied that the means adopted to deal with this fear are adequate. This may result in a situation where the effort to deal with the fear of the unknown goes on without any definable limit or norm. One never can say that the fear of the unknown has been addressed and taken care of adequately, and as such, this fear could continue to take away a lot of one's energy and effort both at the conscious and sub-conscious levels."

The lady social worker asked: "Pawan Ji, we never realized that fear is driving us like this. Can you please also explain how it affects us in our day-to-day lives?"

Pawan Ji said: "This is a very good question. The significant practical effect of this fear complex is that it materially alters our thoughts, our actions, and our life in this world. Fear affects our attitude towards others, our own thinking process, our responses to the situation around us, and our actions in everyday life. Our thoughts and actions would be different if fear was not affecting our minds. Since we let fear to be with us, we live with fear. Fear then affects our lives and the way we live."

Pawan Ji then asked: "Can anyone of you tell us how you see the effect of fear on your life?"

The lady teacher volunteered, and said: "There are many far-reaching effects of fear, and I can think of some that are quite important."

When Pawan Ji encouraged her to elaborate, she continued: "Let me mention three significant effects of fear. First, fear does not allow us to live in the present. We keep worrying about the future. And when we do that, we somehow keep on projecting the past into the future. If anything has gone wrong in the past, we project the same into our future, and then worry about that. We are not able to live in the present moment, and time keeps slipping away. Due to our fear complex, we are either brooding about the past or worrying about the future. I think that badly affects the quality of our life from day-to-day."

"Two, I think our search for power and control also arises from our fear of insecurity in our lives. In our effort to protect ourselves, we try to gain power and control things, even if they may not actually be under our control. I have seen people who are almost mad for acquiring power – whether it is money power or political power. According to me, they are actually suffering from a fear of insecurity. I don't think they are chasing that power for serving others or for some other noble cause. They are doing it due to their fear complex. Actually, things get much worse when their ego and fear combine. Then it becomes pure lust for power, and quickly degenerates into greed and exploitation."

She had obviously got worked up and the agitation was reflected in her voice.

She paused, regained her composure, and continued: "The third point is about the effect of fear on our responses and relationships. Because of fear, we often create an image in our mind about the negative side of situations or of persons we have to deal with. These images are created on the basis of a past experience or event which was not what we wanted or liked. Whether we carry this at our conscious level or sub-conscious level, we are afraid of the same thing happening again in future. Our responses then get conditioned to address that apprehended situation, even though that does not exist, and may never exist. The same thing happens with our interpersonal relationships. We keep looking at situations and relationships with colored glasses of fear in our mind; and then, our responses get distorted."

She looked at us and seemed quite relaxed to see that everyone in the room was carefully listening to her.

Encouraged by our full attention to her, she continued: "It may look odd, but in many cases, not only our responses but our relationships are also based upon fear instead of respect, affection or emotions. For instance, in our families, many children are motivated to behave or do things for fear of punishment by the teacher or the parent. In our workplace, many subordinates choose to perform for fear of their boss, rather than a sense of duty or desire to do the right thing. What kind of relationships can you expect between them, if these are based upon fear? Can you believe, even when it comes to our relationship with God, how many times we are told to fear God? I have never understood why God would want us to fear Him, instead of loving Him?"

This was becoming quite interesting.

The young man who was a business executive wanted to share his experience, and said: "I work for a large business group. I had assumed that we were expected to run business and industry for producing goods and services, which would help everyone, live a better life, and within that process, we were justified in making good profits for ourselves. But I am somewhat disillusioned when I see that acquiring wealth is all that matters now. Sometimes, maximum wealth is created by a business, which is far removed from actual production of goods and services. I do not want to name them, but they seem to control and run the money-making process whether in the financial world of stock markets or in the domain of government control and license and quota regime. This goes on as a never-ending process and is constantly driven by greed. I do not know why there should be so much greed and amassing of wealth, but I am inclined to believe that fear and insecurity have a lot to do with this."

He probably realized the need to clarify his statement, and added: "I do not mean that everyone in business and industry is driven by greed and a fear of insecurity. There are many exceptions, and there are many examples of good business houses working for economic growth for the benefit of everyone. But barring these exceptions, the money-making process is basically driven by greed and an underlying fear of insecurity, even though both these factors may not be explicitly recognized and may remain at the sub-conscious level of the people."

As I listened to him, I realized for the first time how much influence was exerted by fear upon us and upon the ways of the world in which we live and work.

Pawan Ji took over, and said in his soothing voice: "This situation is not desirable. Living in fear does us no good. But if we understand this, let me ask you, why should we then keep living in fear?"

All of us were trying to find the answer. Everyone remained silent.

Pawan Ji waited for a while, and then posed further questions for us to think about.

He questioned: "Do we really need this fear complex? Does it serve some useful or strategic purpose in life? For instance, does the fear complex enable us or help us in our survival or for achieving success in the world, or in protecting ourselves or our possessions? That could be so, if it was found that but for the fear, the safeguards would not have been there, and the likely loss or damage would have gone unchecked. Or if it was found, that but for the fear and insecurity, a person would not work at his or her best and would not achieve all that is possible."

Pawan Ji said in a rather firm tone: "Obviously, that is not so. On the contrary, you may find that fear compromises one's ability and initiative to move forward freely and do things in the best possible manner – that is to say, without fear or favor. Fear may hold the person back and may make him adopt an attitude which is unduly defensive and much less than the optimum. Then, fear would work as a negative force in your life."

"How then, should we decide whether we should live with or without fear? Where is the dividing line to keep the fear in – or out of – our life?" he asked.

Pawan Ji was looking at us intently to see our reactions.

He paused, and then said in his comforting voice: "Each one of us needs to find an answer to this question. I will not say anything more about this question of fear. I leave this to each one of you to decide for yourself. All I wish to say is that you should become aware of your fear complex, so that you can then deal with it."

He then moved on to explain how the third element, namely our belief system, has conditioned our Outer-me. Before doing that, he looked at me and asked if I would like to tell everyone what our belief system is.

I took over, and said: "Our education, our experiences in life and our socially-accepted norms make up our belief system. This becomes a set of beliefs which we take for granted and continue to live with and act on that basis in our lives. Many of these beliefs run from generation to generation, family to family, and society to society and become the accepted parameters for our conduct and behavior in our workplace and in our inter-personal interactions."

Pawan Ji asked me: "Can you spell out what are the major beliefs which we have adopted as part of our belief system."

I responded: "There are so many of them, and these also keep changing from time to time. Let me just point out a few of these which have material effect on our thinking and our responses in our daily lives."

"The first belief we acquire and carry with us is that each one of us exists as a separate individual and there is a separate world which exists around us. In other words, we believe that we are the subjects and the world is an object of our experience. This builds up a notion of separation between me and the world, and also between me and every other person. This notion of separateness makes it difficult for us to see the reality of our own self and the world in its holistic perspective. We see only bits and pieces of it and not the whole picture, and therefore end up with a fragmented view of the situations arising before us. We also lose sense of our inter-connectivity with others both at physical and emotional levels. All our relationships and responses are worked out on this basis."

I continued: "This notion of separateness inevitably leads us to an urge to control and dominate the world. We then strive to control not only others living in the world, but also the nature around us. This urge to dominate others and the nature often degenerates into an urge to exploit them for our own advantage or gain. This becomes a part of our belief system and conditions our responses accordingly."

I wanted to explain further, and added: "Two related beliefs follow from this first belief of our separateness. When we accept the belief that each one is a separate and unconnected person, we come to believe that each one must compete with the other in order to succeed in the world. To justify this notion, we even work out theories to show that such competition is desirable to bring out the best in every person, and this is good for everyone. We then adopt competition as our guiding principle instead of adopting mutual cooperation as the basis of our actions and relationships. This has a very far-reaching effect on our responses in those situations."

"Another related belief that is built up on the basis of the same premise of separateness is the belief in hierarchy. This divides us into classes and categories of higher and lower levels of hierarchy. This happens in almost all contexts of our interpersonal relationships, including those within a family, or in places of work, or in social and political systems. This not only reinforces the notion of separateness but creates divisions amongst us, and these divisions affect our responses in those situations."

I had been speaking long enough, and thought it best to stop.

Pawan Ji expressed his appreciation and said: "Aparna has shown to us a very clear picture of our belief systems and their effect on our responses at the level of our Outer-me. To sum up, our Outer-me, and our responses in the outside world are conditioned by three main factors, namely, our ego, our fear complex, and our belief systems. You must have noted that our Inner-me is normally not conditioned by these factors and therefore, can remain quite different from our Outer-me."

I wanted a clarification and asked Pawan Ji: "There are many qualities and characteristics of an individual which may be inherent from birth, either because these are genetic or inherited otherwise. Do these also form part of our ego or belief systems?"

Pawan Ji replied: "Yes, these genetic or inherited traits do become part of the Outer-me. But they do not form part of our ego and belief systems which cause a difference between the Outer-me and Inner-me."

Then he looked at me and asked: "Aparna, you are a gynecologist and you see so many babies arriving in this world. As you very well know, a newborn baby has certain instincts – like instincts for self-preservation, love and happiness. You can observe the self-preservation instinct in his reflexes, his instinct for happiness in his smile, and his instinct for love in his response to the mother. Tell me, have you ever seen a newborn baby having an ego, fear or a belief system? If this is not so, it is obvious that all these are acquired later in life from the external influences and environment, and then become part of the Outer-me."

He continued: "On the other hand, the basic nature of Inner-me is peace and love – not ego, nor fear, nor beliefs acquired in the external world."

He concluded: "My purpose in this workshop was to make you all aware of your Outer-me and your Inner-me and the influence of these three factors upon the Outer-me. I also wanted you to understand how these factors affect your responses to different situations that come up before you. I hope you have a good idea of this now."

He then gave us a 15-minute break for tea and coffee.

When we re-assembled, Pawan Ji showed us an interesting diagram projected on the screen in the conference room. It showed a human figure in the middle, with two reflections of the figure on either side, one marked Inner-me and the other marked Outer-me. Outer-me was connected with three arrows to Ego, Fear and Belief System. All these three were then inter-connected and then connected to a square-marked Responses and this square was in turn connected to a circle marked Happiness and Unhappiness. On the other side of the diagram, Inner-me was connected to Equilibrium and then, to another square marked Responses, and this was then connected to the same circle marked Happiness and Unhappiness.

He explained these inter-connections and it became easy for us to visualize these with the help of the diagram appearing on the screen. It looked like this:

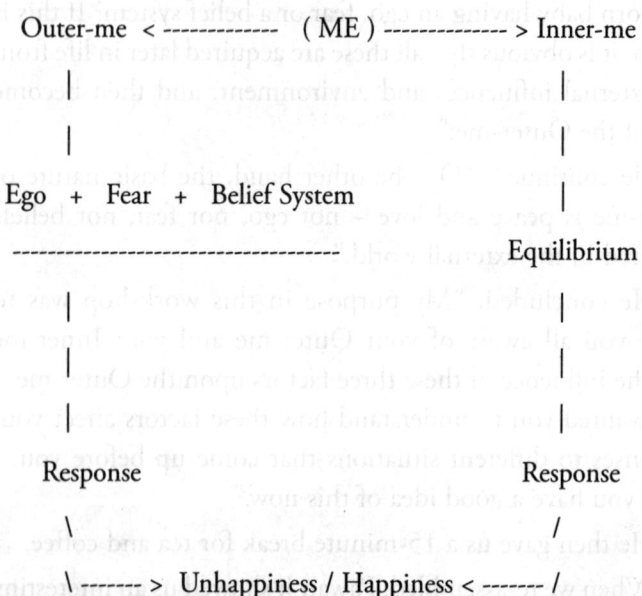

In summary, this diagram showed that our personality has two faces, one Outer-me and the other Inner-me. The

Outer-me is conditioned by three main factors – Ego, Fear and our Belief System. These then become the basis for the responses of our Outer-me to the situations arising in life. These responses result in happiness or unhappiness for the person in those situations, depending upon the extent to which these are positively or negatively conditioned and driven by the three factors, namely our ego, fear and belief system.

The other side of the diagram showed a similar relationship for Inner-me, except that at the first level, there was no intervention of ego, fear and belief system in generating the responses. Pawan Ji explained that this was so because these three factors come into play in the outer world, and our Inner-me does not get conditioned by them. As such, an enlightened Inner-me can remain in a state of equilibrium and thus provide the appropriate responses which will lead to happiness.

Pawan Ji further pointed out that following from this analysis, two conclusions could be drawn:

One, wherever our Outer-me is at work, unhappiness in life can be avoided if we remain fully aware of our ego, fear and belief systems and we prevent these from exerting a negative influence on our responses to the situations before us.

Two, if we can choose our Inner-me to prevail over our Outer-me whenever practically possible we can respond from a state of equilibrium and avoid the problem of wrong responses and consequent unhappiness in our life.

Things were becoming quite clear to me and I felt that I had found my answers. Now I knew how to be my own self – both at the level of Outer-me dealing with my actions and relationships in the world outside, and Inner-me dealing with my world of thoughts and emotions inside. I no longer have to live as a divided self and I can see the inter-connection and harmony at both levels of my existence. I had been searching for this unity and harmony for a long time, and today I had found them. It was a great feeling – as if clouds had been cleared from a hazy sky, and finally I was able to see its clear blue expanse and the light that shines beyond.

My thoughts were interrupted when someone from our group asked: "Pawan Ji, your presentation is very nice and helpful. Basically it tells me that I am better off living at the level of Inner-me for my own self and my own happiness. Is that possible, and what happens if I do that?"

Pawan Ji smiled and responded: "Before I answer your question, I wish to clarify one thing. As I said at the beginning, Outer-me and Inner-me are two aspects or two faces of your own self. One is engaged in action in the outside world and the other works inside you, but they are totally inter-connected. The difference in the two arises because of the three factors we have just now discussed, namely, your ego, your fear complex and your belief system. These become part of your Outer-me but do not normally enter your Inner-me. It would therefore, follow that if you disregard these three factors, you start living for all purposes and in all situations at Inner-me, or as close to that as possible. As I also clarified earlier, because of the compulsions of Outer-me, you may not be able to totally give up one or more of these three factors. But it is enough if you develop full awareness that these do exist within your Outer-me. That awareness will enable you to stay clear of the negative effect which these factors may otherwise have on your responses."

He continued: "So, to answer the first part of your question, I say that it is possible for you to move away from Outer-me and come as close as possible to your Inner-me. Obviously, that would enable you also to move away from the influences of these three factors – ego, fear and belief system – on your responses as much as possible."

"To answer the second part of your question, let me say that if you are interested in discovering your real self and the meaning and purpose of your life and existence, you should begin a new journey at the level of Inner-me. Once you begin this journey, a kind of transformation starts taking place in your mind and attitude. You start searching for substance, instead of looking at the form of things. The things, which earlier seemed so important, the relationships which looked so indispensable, and priorities for which you worked so hard all this time, will now appear in a new light. Perhaps, for the first time you will realize that you can observe and examine them rather than becoming a part of them, or being trapped by them."

"You may also realize that your happiness is not found in them, nor dependent on them. As the journey continues, realization comes that happiness is to be found not in something existing or happening outside, but your happiness lies in how you respond to these. Then, all the external things, events and situations are at best the trigger points or causes, but by themselves do not carry or give happiness. Your happiness or unhappiness arises from your own responses to them. This could be a very liberating revelation in as much as, you suddenly become aware of the source of happiness that lies within your own self, and to that extent, you become free from dependence on the events at the level of Outer-me."

There was complete silence, as everyone in our group was trying to absorb all that had been said.

In that moment, I thought of Raj and wished he could

have come with me to attend this workshop. The journey that Pawan Ji was talking about was something that I would very much like to begin not alone by myself, but along with him.

When I mentioned this to Pawan Ji, he laughed and summed up his final thoughts and his answer to my question, in beautiful words: "A journey becomes more joyful if we can travel with someone who shares the same path and looks for the same destination. If we keep our eyes and ears open, it should be possible to find that someone. This could be your spouse, a relative or a friend. It is quite probable that someone is already somewhere around you. All that may be needed is to open your mind and look for that someone. Mutual interaction between the two persons can then be very delightful if they can share their vision and approach. Then the journey itself can become a great experience."

He further elaborated: "One must however, recognize that this journey is very much at the level of Inner-me, and therefore, different from anything at the level of Outer-me. While this is happening, Outer-me may continue to interact in the external world, and the real journey may continue at the level of Inner-me. Therefore, it is important that the beliefs and expectations built up or acquired at the Outer-me level cannot and should not be imported or applied at the Inner-me level."

In conclusion, Pawan Ji said: "With this clarity and composure, the journey at Inner-me level would lead to a new discovery, a new vision, and a delightful new level of existence for one's own self. Life would then move to a different level of happiness, and become free from the stress and strain which otherwise seem unavoidable when Outer-me dominates. A new chapter opens in your life as you move to a different level of existence and awareness."

His words kept ringing in my ears as I reached home that evening.

THAT NIGHT, I told Raj about our discussions at the workshop. I was somewhat pleasantly surprised that he found the concept of Inner-me and Outer-me quite interesting and also realistic. When I explained to him that the differences between these two arose because of our ego, our fear, and our belief systems, he went into the details of each of these. I felt happy that I could share all this with him, and I was reminded of what Pawan Ji had said in his concluding remarks about the joy of exploring this together with someone with similar thoughts. I told Raj that at some opportunity, he should also meet Pawan Ji for a fuller interaction and understanding about this subject.

While we were talking, my thoughts went back to my younger brother Vipin. After he lost his job as Vice-President in a financial services company in America, and then had a divorce from his wife Jennifer, he still remained in America. He was now living in New York as a paying guest with an American family, and was still trying to find a proper job there.

When Raj asked me what was I thinking, I said: "Raj, what we discussed in today's workshop, seems to apply very much to Vipin's present situation."

"Why do you say that?" Raj questioned.

I pointed out: "Don't you think it is Vipin's false ego which is holding him up from moving on to a new chapter in his life? I think he is also suffering from a fear complex at his sub-conscious level. It seems to me that he is afraid of being seen as a failure in his recent difficult time, and he is not letting it go."

Raj kept quiet. He was thinking about what I had said.

I added: "I can also see that he is hanging on to his one belief which is not necessarily valid any more. As you know, America has always presented a vision of a land of great opportunity for success in the material world. Anyone who goes there carries a belief that he or she must be able to achieve great material success there. Even though the whole economic situation in America has now radically changed for the worse, this belief seems to persist. I think Vipin is also living under the same old belief, even now."

Raj could see the point, but asked: "Do you mean that his Outer-me is dominating, and exerting upon him the influence of ego, fear, and a cherished belief which is no longer valid? If this is so, he certainly needs to become aware of these and do something to get rid of them."

He thought for a moment, and asked: "Can anyone explain this to him, and make him see things in a different light?"

I replied: "Why not? We can try. Let us talk to him and see how he responds. It has been quite a while since I last spoke to him."

Considering a time difference of just over ten hours between Delhi and New York, this was just the right time to make a phone call to Vipin. He answered the phone and sounded pleasantly surprised to hear my voice. I had activated the speaker phone on our system so that both Raj and I could listen and talk. The conversation went on quite well.

"Hi Vipin, how are you doing? We miss you so much." I told him.

"I miss you too. I am Ok. How are you? Is Raj running around as ever, trying to make even more money from his clients?" He asked in a lighter vein.

Raj spoke: "It is your sister who makes me work so hard. She gives all her time to her hospital and her patients. Not much for me. So I have no choice but to devote all my time to work. I think I would be better off being her patient, rather than her husband."

I intervened: "Vipin, never believe a lawyer. He is a good lawyer, and he can twist the facts anytime. Yes, both of us are busy. But we have no complaints."

Vipin had a good laugh, and asked: "Is this why you have phoned – for me to listen to you fight?"

I said: "No. I want to know if you have found a new job. What are you doing?"

He became cautious, and said: "Nothing has been finalized as yet but I have three possible openings. Today I had a good meeting at J B Holzman's office. They are one of the top financial services firms. With the new policy and the relief package rolled out by President Obama the situation here is likely to improve. Something should work out for me pretty soon. Don't worry. I am doing all that needs to be done. Just send me your good wishes."

I was touched, and spoke out: "Vipin, you are always on our minds, and all our good wishes are with you. But we want to talk to you about some more practical ways of handling the situation that you are facing."

"Yes. What do you want to say?" He asked.

Raj was listening, and kept quiet.

I then said: "Vipin, you should move forward. You should

see that the entire situation has changed, both in your personal life and in your financial services world. I think, you should take a fresh look, and not persist with the past."

"I am not persisting with the past. I am trying to work out things all over again. What more can I do?" He asked.

"No. As I see it, your past is holding you up. Let it go, and move on. There is so much more that you can do in life." I tried to convince him.

He paused, and said with some frustration in his voice: "I don't understand. If you think you know, tell me what my problem is, and what is holding me up, and from what?"

Raj gestured to me to calm down. I took the hint, and said in a soft tone: "Vipin, I have been exploring such situations to understand their causes and cures. Let me say, your present situation has happened for reasons beyond your control. I certainly do not, and cannot, blame you for that. This can happen to anyone. What is important is how you respond to that now." I was trying hard to explain my point of view.

He seemed receptive, and asked: "Ok. I am responding as best I can. Tell me, what is wrong with that."

I took the opportunity, and said: "I am very happy that you say so. But as I see it, there are three things which are coming in the way of your giving a proper response."

He kept quiet, waiting for me to continue, and I continued: "Vipin, you seem to have cultivated an image of yourself and your cherished career in the financial world. As you know, for whatever reasons, that image has not turned out to be a reality. But you are not letting it go. As I see it, that has become your ego, and that is not your real position today. Unless you give up this ego, you would not be able to move forward to a new life."

Raj tried to stop me from saying all this. But I knew Vipin was listening, and I did not want to miss the opportunity to help him see the reality.

I continued in a very soft tone: "Vipin, please do not have any fear in your mind. A fear complex will prevent you from facing the world and giving the right response. Why should you be afraid of what people will think if you give up the old model which has not worked out for you? And why should you be afraid of taking up a new path in your life now? There is no reason for you to be afraid of calling it quits and coming back to your home country to start afresh, if that is the correct and sensible thing to do." I tried to explain.

He was completely silent, and I had to ask if he was able to hear me. When he said "Yes", I continued: "Vipin, your old belief in America as the ultimate haven for success in the material world, is also not valid any more. You know the situation there. So don't let this belief hold you up from taking a fresh look at the reality as it exists now."

Raj thought it necessary to intervene, and said: "Vipin, I understand how difficult it is to handle these situations in life. I think you are handling it with great confidence. Don't mind what Aparna is telling you. It is her style. I have to live with that all the time. Now, even when you are thousands of miles away, you also have to live with that."

Vipin laughed, and said in a humorous way: "Raj, now you know why I am not in a hurry to come back!"

We all had a good laugh.

Vipin was obviously relaxed, and said: "Aparna, you have become very smart. I think, what you say makes a lot of sense. I will see if my ego, my hidden fear, and some old beliefs, are working in my mind consciously or unconsciously. Actually, I had never thought about these. But now that you have pointed out, I will of course look into these. Maybe this will open up a new phase in my life and will enable me to move forward free from my past. Let me think."

He paused, and then said lovingly: "Aparna, you mean so much to me. I do want to come and see you and Raj at the earliest opportunity. Let me see when it becomes possible. Good bye for now."

"Good bye and best wishes from both of us," we responded.

We closed our phone call, and perhaps, opened up a new vision for my brother.

CHAPTER 5

Where are you going?

I WAS INVITED TO present a paper at an international conference in Singapore on the subject of hormonal therapy for women. This was a frequently recurring issue for women who had undergone surgery for removal of ovaries or who were facing post-menopausal syndromes. I had done considerable work in this area, and I was looking forward to update myself at this conference on this subject.

I had checked-in at the Singapore Airlines counter in Delhi airport and was waiting in the lounge for my flight to Singapore. This was an early morning flight and I had closed my eyes, trying to make up for lost sleep.

"Hey, where are you going?" I heard a familiar voice asking me. I opened my eyes and saw Air Chief OP Mehra smiling. He sat down beside me with his cup of tea.

In that brief moment as I tried to be fully awake, I found myself slightly disoriented. What was he asking? Do I know where I am going? What can I say?

Before I could speak, he said: "I am on the same flight. Are you also going to Singapore, or somewhere beyond?"

Oh, so he did not mean to ask what I had thought. I relaxed, and told him that I was going to Singapore to attend a conference and I would be there for the next three days.

He said: "In that case, you must come and join us tomorrow evening for a dinner we are hosting to celebrate the 25th wedding anniversary of my daughter. They will be happy to see you. I am inviting you, and you must come".

I had known the Air Chief's daughter since her childhood. She and her husband had been living in Singapore for many years. I would surely like to see them on this happy occasion. I readily accepted the invitation.

The flight was announced for boarding. We were both in business class, and the cabin crew was very helpful in getting our seats next to one another. As I settled down in my seat and closed my eyes, Air Chief's words flashed through my mind, and many questions cropped up: Where am I going? I know that this flight is going to Singapore, but do I know where am I going? And why am I going wherever I am going? Do I know my destination? Where is my life taking me? Do I even know where I am right now? And if I know that, why do I want to go somewhere else? Why, and where? So many questions were coming up in my mind.

I was tired and wanted to sleep. I asked the airhostess to put a do-not-disturb sign on my seat headrest. I had a short nap. When I woke up, we were served a very nice brunch – a combination of breakfast and lunch – courtesy of Singapore airlines. We both enjoyed the brunch. After that, the air hostess brought us very tempting chocolate ice cream. I didn't want that, but Air Chief pressed me and said: "Aparna, you are young and you can afford it. Take it, and it will make you happy."

I shot back mischievously: "Ice cream cannot make me happy. It is only my response to it that can do so, and I don't feel like responding well to ice cream at this time!"

He smiled and looked quite amused.

And I added: "Uncle, you told me that – didn't you?"

He had a big laugh, and said: "Yes, I did. But I didn't know that you had picked it up so well. Aparna, I always knew you were smart, but now you are really getting smarter!"

We started talking and I told him about Pawan Ji and the workshop I had attended at his healthcare center. I also told him about the concepts of Outer-me and Inner-me and their interesting implications on our responses and happiness.

He was very appreciative and said: "I am really happy that you are putting these ideas into practice. Knowledge is of no use if not utilized in your daily life."

And then he asked me: "Aparna, why do you look so tired? What is the problem?"

I was touched by his concern for me, and I told him: "Uncle, I am just overworked. There are so many small things at the hospital and I have to get involved in these, even though these are routine jobs. I don't see why I have to do all that. But you have been in so many high positions, like Governor, Chairman, and Chief of Air Force. How did you handle all these big and small things coming up before you?"

He smiled, looked at me and said: "I will answer you in two parts. First, I never considered anything too small for me to handle. Even a small thing going wrong can upset the entire process. Can you imagine the consequence if even a small part or process in an aircraft goes wrong? So, every little thing is important to me. It does not mean that I have to do everything myself, but I am surely responsible for it. Second, even if a thing looks small, I always look at it in the perspective of the larger mission or objective. That takes away any frustration of dealing with things which seem too small to be dealt with by me if I see them in isolation."

For me, this was an altogether new perspective of looking at my work and responsibility. It sounded so positive and helpful.

He then added: "Let me tell you an interesting story. A wise man was walking past a construction site where many workers were engaged in digging the foundation. As he saw one worker digging the earth with his shovel, he asked what he was doing.

The worker responded with some degree of annoyance: "Why do you ask? Can't you see I am digging the earth, and I have to do it in the burning heat of sun?"

The wise man walked over to another worker doing a similar job. When he asked him the same question, the worker replied: "Sir, I have a family to support, and I am doing all this to earn my living. Don't we all have to do that?"

As the wise man moved on to another worker with a shovel in his hand and doing similar work, he asked him the same question. The worker replied with a smile: "Sir, you must be a great man. I want to tell you that they are building a temple here and we are working to make that temple."

The Air Chief stopped, and wanted me to draw my own conclusions. I was struck with the impact of this story. It told me that it is a matter of our own perception that makes all the difference in our attitudes and responses. Once again, I realized how our different responses in similar situations can lead to totally different experiences for us. It also dawned on me why we need to see things and actions not in isolation but in their holistic dimension – as integral constituents of the whole and not as mere separate parts.

I told the Air Chief that the story was indeed very meaningful and instructive.

I wanted to know more about the subject and asked him for a clarification: "Uncle, this is wonderful. Can you also help me understand how I can develop the holistic perspective that would enable me to see the whole – and not just a part of a situation?"

He was quite willing to explain, and said: "I will tell you how I do that. This is something you do at the level of your own consciousness and in your own mind – not something for which you have to look to someone else. Usually, we are accustomed to looking at and connecting with things or situations within a narrow framework which exists in our mind. This limits our perception and we see them within that narrow framework. If we want to see and connect with the whole, we need to expand our own consciousness and go beyond that narrow framework."

"OK. I am listening and trying to understand. Can you explain, what do you mean by expanding our consciousness?" I asked.

He said: "Let me give you another example to show how you can do it in actual practice.

Assume that you are sitting in the living room in your home, and you get a phone call on your mobile. The person asks you where you are at that time. Now you can say, I am in the living room. When you say this, you have defined and connected yourself mentally at that moment with the living room and its four walls. But, you could very well say, I am in my home; and then you have expanded your mind and connected yourself with the entire home and not just the living room. Similarly, you could have responded by saying that you were in a particular colony, or a particular city, or a particular country. Each of these statements is correct, but each defines a different limit of your perceived connection."

"As you expand your mind to connect with progressively larger frameworks, your own consciousness expands to connect with the whole at that higher level. As you can see, it is possible to move from a lower level to a higher level of whole, without any need for you to actually remove the physical boundaries of your living room or your colony or city or country. You are still sitting in the same place but your expanded consciousness connects you to the larger picture. This is what I do. This is my way of expanding my consciousness to connect with the whole at each successive higher level of reality around me."

He thought for a while, and then continued: "Let me add, just as this applies to the situations arising before me, it applies equally well to the relationships in my life. For example, when you think about relationships, you can see and describe yourself as an individual all by yourself, or as an integral part of a larger family, or as a member of a team in a business corporation, or as a member of a particular community or society, or as a citizen of a nation. Each of these descriptions will place you in a different level of relationship with others and you will connect at a different level of the whole situation or relationship. The wider your perspective, the more connected you will be at the holistic level instead of remaining at a fragmented level. I must say, this has worked very well for me, and has always helped me to handle situations and relationships in a larger perspective. You also can easily do this."

As I listened to him with full attention, I considered myself to be really fortunate to have a person of his eminence and knowledge to guide me in my life. I also thanked my good luck for being on this flight and having the opportunity to spend this time with him.

The air hostess had drawn the window shades down and turned off the main lights in the cabin. There were another three hours of flight to go; we both closed our eyes to get some rest. After about an hour or so, the drink service in the cabin commenced and we helped ourselves to cups of very good

Colombian coffee. The rest had done me a lot of good and I felt quite relaxed.

I looked at the Air Chief, and even at his age, he looked quite fit and relaxed, and had a soft glow on his face. I could not help asking him the secret of that.

He was amused, and said: "Aparna, I thought you were a good doctor. So, you would know the secret of good health. As far as I know, the secret lies in freedom – a freedom to do things that one wants to do, and in the manner one likes to do them. Do you agree with that?"

I responded: "Yes, of course, that is very important. But where do we find that freedom? We are totally bogged down with rules, regulations, restrictions and limitations at every step in our life. These come up from all sides, and are imposed on us not only for our own conduct and behavior but for almost everything that we can or cannot do."

He was listening with interest, and I continued: "We virtually have become prisoners of the systems in which we have to live and work. Unfortunately, these systems themselves have become inadequate and inefficient. You can see that situation when you look at our social and political systems, which are not only outdated and inefficient but are marred by so much corruption. It is we who have to suffer for all this."

He thought for a moment, and then said: "There are two possible ways of handling this problem. One, we should work at changing the systems and all the rules and restrictions that go with them. But this can only be done by a collective will and joint effort of all the people, and this is a rather long-drawn process. Two, at your personal level and within a short-term horizon, you need to find your own solution. That may be difficult at the level of your Outer-me, but it is quite feasible at the level of your Inner-me that you explained to me earlier. If you can be free at the level of your Inner-me, you can avoid the frustration and unhappiness for yourself."

I was curious to know how this could be done at the level of Inner-me without waiting for the systems and the rules to change.

When I asked him, he said: "Let me explain this by another example. This morning you came to the airport in your car from your home, and as you drove down, you had to follow all the rules and regulations, like driving on the left, keeping within the speed limits, staying clear of road dividers and pavements, and stopping at traffic lights. But once you boarded the plane and your plane was flying a few thousand feet above the ground, you could see down below all the traffic caught up in the same rules and restrictions, but you had risen above them. While all the rules and restrictions continued to remain as they were, you had risen higher and these no longer affected you. I would say the rules and restrictions remained where they were, but you transcended them."

He explained further: "It is a somewhat similar situation when you move to your Inner-me and live at that level. You have then risen above the level of your Outer-me and you are in a position to transcend and to live without being bogged down by all those limitations of the external world. This can give you your own freedom and save you from frustration and tension in your life. You still follow the world at the level of Outer-me, but you are free at the level of Inner-me."

I was curious and asked: "Uncle, has this really worked for you?"

"Yes, and I see no reason why it cannot work for you as

well." He replied, and then jokingly added: "You are smarter than me, any time. So you can make it work better."

I did not know how to respond, but I did say: "Yes I am smarter than you because I have found someone like you to guide me, and you have not been able to find anyone like that for yourself."

He laughed, and affectionately patted me on my back: "Ok, Aparna, you are smart, and you have the last word on everything. I concede."

That was the most memorable flight I ever had.

Once in Singapore, I got busy with the conference. I met him the next evening at dinner at his daughter's home. We had a very pleasant time that evening. The next day, I returned back to Delhi.

BACK HOME, I found there was an invitation to Raj and I from Dr. Sonali of the Parmarth Ashram in Rishikesh. This was for a function the next Sunday for inauguration of a new eye hospital at the Ashram. The inauguration was to be done by the Governor of the State, a large number of distinguished guests including prominent doctors were expected to be present, and Swami Ji had asked Sonali to invite us for the occasion. Sunday was my day off at the hospital, but Raj had to go to Mumbai for his meetings for a case starting in the court the following Monday. So, I went alone.

I was happy to be at the Ashram once again, and pleasant memories of my previous visit were revived. It turned out to be a grand function. I was pleasantly surprised to see a galaxy of prominent persons from all walks of life were present at the function. This showed the great respect and goodwill built up for the Ashram over the years for its services in the spiritual field and humanitarian causes.

After the inauguration was over, we went round the new hospital and were happy to see that the equipment and facilities were world-class. The doctors working at the hospital were highly qualified and experienced and had opted to work there obviously with a motivation for service.

Swami Ji had agreed to deliver a lecture that afternoon. Sonali recommended that I hear him; and that turned out to be a great experience for me.

It was a big gathering of more than 500 people. Swami Ji was dressed in his usual saffron clothing and radiated an aura of life force around him.

After the initial invocation for peace, he spoke slowly in a soft voice: "Today we have dedicated a new eye hospital at the Ashram for the service of everyone. I am quite pleased that you all have joined to support this noble cause. Many of you have come from far off places. This shows your dedication and commitment to render humanitarian service. I am happy that you are holding on to your values in life. I know that is not easy, but you are doing it – and doing it quite well. May God bless you."

He then continued: "But many a times, questions may arise in your mind about the meaning and purpose of all this work, and about the reason why you should be doing that while living in this world. I want to tell you about one such question. This morning, before the start of the function for dedicating the hospital, a very intelligent young man came to me and asked: "Swami Ji, we are often told by our spiritual masters that the world is a temporary illusion or Maya, it is not real, and it is not going to last. Why are you then making all these Ashrams and hospitals if everything is just an illusion? Why should we spend all our life working so hard to build up all these things in this world?"

"I can see that many of you may have a similar question in your mind. So, let us look into this. First of all, I want to make it very clear that our Vedanta and Upanishads, which are the ultimate repository of our ancient spiritual knowledge, do not say that this world is unreal or a mirage."

To prove the point, he added: "Let me quote the very first line of the first shloka in Kathopnishad. It says: "Ishwavasyamidam sarvam yat kincham jagatyam jagat". This literally means that whatever exists in this entire world is a manifestation of the same supreme divine force."

He continued: "I can give you many references in other scriptures that assert the same truth. Therefore, the scriptures do not mean to say that this world is an illusion or unreal. What the scriptures say is that what appears before us is not permanent. It is the external form of things that appears before us. This form is not permanent and is constantly undergoing change. It is in this sense that the impermanence of the world is in its form, which appears before us, and not in its substance which manifests the divine force.

"You must understand this carefully. All things in the world change with time. Natural surroundings change, man-made structures change, social and political systems change, and your own body and mind change. The change is happening at all levels all the time. Sometimes the change is slow, sometimes it is fast, and sometimes it is so massive that a thing in its present form may disperse or dissolve and take up an entirely new form."

Swami Ji further elaborated: "What the scriptures are saying is that the form which you see is impermanent and will not remain the same. But there is no denial that the world is a creation and manifestation of the same supreme divine force – the same supreme power which has created you and which sustains you through your life. Therefore, please remember that the world is real but its form is impermanent and will change. That applies to everything in the world around you – and equally to your own body."

"What the scriptures therefore ask you is: recognize and deal with this change, focus on the substance, and don't be caught up in the form which will not last forever. There could be two possible ways for you to deal with this constantly changing mode of the world. One-way is that you may try to exercise control and domination over things and their process of change. Since the change is happening at all levels, this would require you to devise and adopt ways and means of controlling and dominating human beings as well as nature and their change process. Science and technology have been doing this for you for ages. I need not go into the consequences of this approach; and we are regularly reminded of these by the phenomena of exploitation and oppression in human societies and ecological disasters in the nature around us.

Swami Ji moved on to the second point, and said: "The other way is to facilitate and assimilate the change. Facilitating would mean that you understand and guide the change in the desired direction, and make the change process as efficient and smooth as possible. In certain situations, you may not only participate but may even lead the change as part of your facilitation process. Whether you participate in the change or lead it, in both cases, you need to understand the forces, which are at work. You need to harmonize your responses with these forces, instead of trying to control or dominate them or trying to resist them. You will find it better to more or less flow with them and to adopt an approach to direct them in the desired direction rather than fighting against them. The energy of those forces then works for you. This will save you a lot of energy and effort which would otherwise be wasted if you are in confrontation. Let me also add that if you work against these forces, it will not only be challenging but may eventually turn out to be a losing battle."

"This is not very difficult to do. In a way, you are already following this approach, but now you need to consciously make it a part of your responses in your daily life. For example, when you drive on the road, you harmonize your movement with the traffic as it flows. You will encounter problems if you go either too slow or too fast or against the traffic. The same holds good whether you are flying an aeroplane, or you are swimming in a river. You need to go with the forces, not against them. You must understand that you are a part of a much larger cosmic network, which is operating according to the laws of nature and very powerful forces at work. Your intelligence lies in understanding these laws and forces and harmonizing your responses with them. You won't achieve much by trying to control or dominate them."

"As you facilitate the change, you assimilate it into your own life. This means that you understand the impact and effect of change, and you make appropriate adjustments or adaptations in your own life and in the situations around you. Again, this is an ongoing process as and when the changes keep on taking place. In fact, you are already making these adjustments and adaptations as you move on in your everyday life. For example, you do this every time you add a new member in your family whether by birth or marriage, or lose one by sickness or death – or you change your job or place of residence, or have a change in your own body due to age or sickness, or face a change in the systems in the external world around you. In each of these cases, you need to assimilate the change by making necessary adjustments or adaptations within yourself, or in your situations. All I am asking is that you should consciously recognize and willingly adopt this assimilation process. You can then do a much better job and free yourself from a lot of tension and unhappiness which may otherwise arise due to your negative response to a change taking place in your situation or a relationship."

"In order to develop the ability for a positive response, you need to accept that change is a necessary part of the process of evolution, and assimilating the change is a good step in that process. Our culture recognizes this in a beautiful way. We see this as a constant ongoing process of integration and disintegration of all things in the world. Birth and death are also seen as integral parts of this process. In fact, we have three essential and inter-related phases of such constant change. These are – creating, sustaining and dissolving. It is interesting to note that each of these are supposed to be dealt with by a separate manifestation of the Divine Power. Lord Brahma is the creator of our world, Lord Vishnu sustains and runs it, and Lord Shiva dissolves it in order to re-create. In a way, these three phases of change are being dealt with by you in your own life. Every birth is creating, every death is dissolving and all your work in the world is sustaining; and you are living through each of these phases."

"Therefore, the real question before you is not whether the

world is unreal or a mirage, nor why should you work hard to build and create things in the world. The real question is how you should recognize the change in the world around you and in your own self, and deal with that in the best possible way. Obviously, if you do not deal properly with the changing world, you will face failure at every step in your everyday life and end up being unhappy and frustrated."

He paused, and said in a rather firm tone: "Dealing with this constantly changing world is the real issue that every one of us faces in our life, all the time."

Everyone was silently absorbing the impact of Swami Ji's message.

And then Swami Ji added in a very helpful tone: "Our scriptures give us excellent guidance on this issue."

He continued: "In order to understand this, you need to first understand what change does to you. You exist in this world as a human being; and whatever you are at this moment is your present state of Being. When a change happens in or around you, and you assimilate that change, you evolve and move to another state of Being. This process of change takes you from your present state of Being to your new state of Being. Every change does that, howsoever small may be the resulting difference between your states of Being before and after the change. Such differences could be in your physical or mental states, your thoughts or perceptions, or your relationships, or your possessions, or in situations around you, which affect your overall personality and position. After every such change, your prior state of Being becomes another state of Being."

"This transition into another state of Being is your process of Becoming. In your daily life, you are constantly engaged in this process of Becoming – to become someone different and move into another state of Being. All your knowledge, skill and resources are working for this process of Becoming – to bring about a change in your present state of Being whether as per your desires and aspirations or by force of circumstances. Each step of Becoming intends to move your Being from one state to another. Our entire effort in life is devoted to support and to optimize this process of Becoming to achieve this objective.

At every stage, your Being is a state of yourself, and your Becoming is a process in your action. Being is the platform from which Becoming takes off, and Becoming is the process, which transforms the Being into another state. There is a constant interplay-taking place in your life between your Being and Becoming. This is the key to your own evolution in life."

I had closed my eyes in order to fully concentrate and absorb every single word. The message was so clear, and many a doubt or confusion in my mind seemed to have melted away.

Swami Ji continued: "Unfortunately, we are totally caught up in Becoming, and have ignored our Being. We are so engrossed in the process of Becoming that we are constantly chasing and moving from one thing to another in our external world. We have no time to look at our Being, nor for achieving the unity of body and mind and a state of equilibrium. Becoming becomes the focus, Being is forgotten. The process of Becoming then becomes a struggle rather than a process of evolution and smooth transition from one state of Being to another."

"Our scriptures tell you how to deal with your Being and Becoming and achieve a harmonious interplay between these two for best results."

Swami Ji then spoke very slowly: "The ideal state of Being is when body and mind are fully united and both are in a state of equilibrium. This unity of body and mind is achieved by yoga, and equilibrium is achieved by meditation."

"This is neither complicated nor difficult to do."

"When yoga unites your body and mind, all your mental and physical faculties work in unison and harmony. Meditation enables you to screen out the opposing forces, which come upon you from different directions in the world around you. These forces may otherwise have negative influences and may pull and push you in different directions. Meditation allows you to turn away from them and maintain your focused attention and full concentration in a state of equilibrium. Then, you are in a steady state and become like a flame burning upon a candle. When the outside disturbing forces are screened off, the flame is steady and glows in its full glory. Your Being becomes like that flame."

In that state, your Being is in an ideal position to provide the platform for your Becoming to take off. You can experience for yourself that state of Being when you do yoga and meditation. That state of Being is called 'Yogastha' which literally means 'established in yoga'. There is no mystery about it and this does not involve any particular religion or faith. It is universally true for every human being and all you have to do is to learn and practice yoga and meditation."

"Once your Being is established in that state of equilibrium, your process of Becoming comes into action. In that process, the scriptures ask you to detach yourself from worry about the final result and acquire a sense of equanimity. This equanimity means that you detach yourself from any anxiety about the success or failure, while you are engaged in action in the process of your Becoming. You must remember that the scriptures do not ask you to give up the result of your action, but ask you to give up the worry and anxiety for the result when you are engaged in the action. The final result of the action follows in due course, but your equanimity during the action enables you to focus completely on the action. This is called 'Samatvam' which means equilibrium, and this is the key to excellence in action. In that state, the opposing forces do not disturb your action, and it then flows smoothly and efficiently towards excellence in result."

"As you can see very clearly, this approach is practical and pragmatic and opens the door for your own evolution to the highest state of your Being. In simple terms, equilibrium and action are the two key elements for your Being and Becoming."

"Just remember these two key words – Equilibrium and Action – and unite them in practice."

"Let me also point out that if you are searching for the meaning and purpose of your life, this realization and this approach to your Being and Becoming will allow you to find that meaning and purpose."

In conclusion, he said: "Let me sum up all that I have said."

"The key to successful Becoming is positive action to facilitate and assimilate the change in yourself and in the world around you, as time moves on."

"Living life means harmonious blending of your Being and Becoming – instead of confining your focus and attention on one or the other."

"The purpose of your life is the evolution of your Being from its present level to a higher level and eventually, to the highest level."

Swami Ji then blessed us all: "I seek the blessings of the Supreme Divine Power upon each one of you."

"May you Glow like a flame... and Flow like a river..."

"Keep Glowing... Keep Flowing... That's Life."

It was a once-in-lifetime experience for me to listen to these profound words from Swami Ji. There was so much to absorb. No one spoke a word.

We then quietly sat through a five minute meditation.

AFTER THE LECTURE, I returned to my room. Swami Ji's words were forcing me to look at my own life as I was living from day-to-day. Was my Being in a state of unity of my body and mind? Did my Becoming show a coherent and smooth continuity in my life, and was it moving into a clear direction? Or, was my life turning out to be a disjointed sequence of bits and pieces here and there, each depending upon events and circumstances changing from one moment to another? And where did I need to go from here?

My thoughts went back to Pawan Ji's workshop I had attended in Delhi. I tried to focus my thoughts to find the answers, but more questions cropped up in my mind.

Does the reality of the world exist from moment to moment – where each separate moment moves in a time sequence, from the past to the present, and on to the future? Or, does the reality exist as a flow of events – where each previous moment gets transformed into the next and it all becomes a continuous flow? Is life then lived in each discrete moment as an experience specific to that very moment? Or, is life a symphony of our experiences running across time and interwoven with each other?

I realized that the answers to these questions would have a significant bearing on my understanding of life and my experiences in this world. But I still did not know the answers.

I woke up very early next morning as I wanted to have some quiet time to myself. I decided to walk down to the bank of the river Ganges. I found a quiet place on the river-bank and sat there to observe the glory of the river. And as I watched, it seemed to me that the river was so alive that I could feel the energy manifesting itself as the flowing river. I could also feel what the river was symbolizing in its own way.

I felt that the river had an aura of holiness and had its own identity, which was clear and constant. At the same time, every moment, the water was moving away, and fresh water was gushing in and replacing the one before, and there was this constant process of change. I then realized that with such incessant change and water flowing down every moment, one could not hope to enter the same river twice, as it would have changed in the meantime. Nevertheless, despite the changing waters, the river keeps its identity intact; it remains the same river, and continues to quietly assimilate within itself that constant change. That seemed to me just the message for our own lives – the need for assimilating in our lives all the ongoing changes in the world around us, and yet being able to preserve and retain our own identity. I was reminded of what Swami Ji had said in his lecture about facilitating and assimilating the ongoing changes in our life and in the world around us.

I could also see that the river had left its past behind. The river was here, in this very moment, in its full glory – and free from the conditions and places it had moved through in its past. I also felt that it was ready to move on naturally into its future, whatever be the terrain, whatever be the weather, and whichever may be the way forward – whether though cities or wilderness, and whether through mountains or forests. I saw no fear, no worry, no anxiety holding it up – neither for its past nor for its future. The river was here, in this moment, in its natural flow, bubbling with energy, moving with full force, and yet looking calm, composed and serene. What was the river telling me – what was its message for my life?

I also observed that the river appeared to be flowing very fast at some point, and at another point, the water seemed to move rather quietly and slowly. Obviously, this was due to differences in underwater terrain and depth; but I realized that at all points, the river always flowed in the same direction. This was as if the river was telling me that depending upon the conditions in which it had to move forward, it was willing to compromise on its speed, but never on its direction. I could see how true and how pertinent this message was for my own life – to be ready to compromise on the speed, but not on my direction.

I also saw that there were many rocks and boulders in the river bed, which rose above the water, and actually stood in the way of the flowing river. But I did not see the river stopping there, or waiting or trying to remove them. Instead I saw the river always found its way around them, and kept moving on. Again, I could see how very much relevant this was for me living in this world – the river telling me to find and work out my way around such blockades and obstacles, and keep moving forward rather than stopping there or getting into a confrontation with them. This reminded me of the positive action we had talked about in the earlier workshop.

Sitting on the left bank of the river, I could see the right bank on the other side. Despite the great force with which the water was flowing, I noticed that the river was not violating the boundaries of its banks on either side but was maintaining the implicit discipline imposed by the banks on both sides. I realized that if the integrity of the banks were to be violated at any point, the water would spread out and then not only become soiled and dirty, but would also lose direction, and in fact would no longer be the river. Apart from that, it would lead to devastation and damage all around. It then dawned upon me that the social norms and economic and legal systems within which we live are similar to the banks of the river, and these provide the framework for the discipline and direction in our life. Consequences of violating these would not be very different from those for a river if it violates the discipline of its banks within which it is expected to flow.

A thought struck me: where is this river heading to and what is this river's final destination? I could visualize that if it keeps moving in the right direction, it would find its ultimate destination and merge with the ocean. This seemed similar to our spirit eventually finding and merging with the Supreme Divine Power, or becoming one with God. The river knows and accepts its destination, but do we recognize ours? Shouldn't we recognize that, and shouldn't we look forward to that as our ultimate destination, beyond our immediate and short-term goals in life?

But does the journey end there? Does reaching the ocean mean an end for the river? It seemed clear to me that after merging with the ocean, the river will rise again – going up in the form of water vapor into the clouds, raining upon the mountains, and again flowing as a river in its full glory. All of this therefore, is a cyclical process which has neither a beginning nor an end, but is a sequence of various states and events.

Is it not the same for our life? If we recognize our present existence in this world as part of a cyclical process, the events of birth and death take on a very different meaning. Instead of being seen as a beginning and an end of life, these appear as different states and events in the overall process of life in this world. We just move from one state of our existence to another. This is the harmonious interplay of Being and Becoming that Swami Ji had explained in his lecture. Life then appears to flow like a river; and we then also realize that life initially emerges from and eventually merges into the ocean of cosmic force, just like a river.

I felt that the river had shown me many answers. In its own subtle way, the river had highlighted some profound messages for me:

- the need to assimilate all ongoing and recurring changes in my life without losing my identity;
- the joy of living in the present moment without getting caught up in fear or anxiety for the past or future;
- the desirability of remaining flexible in my speed but always maintaining my direction; - the art of exploring and finding my way around the obstacles and blockades that come in my way;
- the merit of abiding by the discipline of social norms and other systems; and
- the wisdom of knowing the destination of the spirit and the meaning of life – as a part of a cyclical process of creation and change.

Above all, the river had shown me that every drop of water in the river is inter-connected, and the story of the river is the story of every single drop of water flowing in it.

That morning, the river had also shown me that life is a continuous flow – and not a summation of isolated experiences in separate moments; and to live in this world, I need to flow with the flow of life.

The cool breeze flowing over the river water was touching my face. It was such a soothing feeling. In that blissful state, I closed my eyes.

Then I felt someone was there, in front of me – and was looking at me. I opened my eyes but no one was there – no one else.

Everything was still, calm, and serene in the soft glow of early morning light just before sunrise. No one else was there.

I slowly closed my eyes again.

It was the river. Yes, it was the river. I heard the river speaking to me.

"My waters keep coming. My waters keep going. But I am not going. I am here all the time."

"In your life, things keep coming, and things keep going. But you are here."

And then it whispered into my ear.

"Where are you going?... It's all here... Right here... Right now."

"Just be aware of yourself – now – in this very moment... Be fearless... And flow with the flow of life."

Notes and References

1. For an in-depth analysis of a 'divided self', see: R. D. Laing, *'The Divided Self'* (1990, Penguin Books, London).
2. Capra, Fritjof, *'The Web of Life'* (1999, Harper Collins Publishers, London), and Capra, Fritjof, *'Uncommon Wisdom'* (1998, Harper Collins Publishers, London).
3. *'Viveka Chudamani'*, translated by Swami Madhavananda (1998, Advaita Ashrama, Calcutta).
4. See: Richard P. Feynman, *'Lectures on Physics'* (1998, Narosa Publishing House, India) vol. I, pp.56, 374.
   Also see:
   - Heisenberg, Werner, *'Physics and Philosophy'* (2000, Penguin Books, UK).
   - Schrodinger, Erwin, *'My View of the World'* (1964, Cambridge University Press, UK).
   - Schrodinger, Werner, *'What is Life'* (2000, Cambridge University Press, UK)
5. For a concise description of these experiments and their implications for wave-particular duality and other quantum characteristics, see: Richard P. Feynman, *'Lectures on Physics'* (1998, Narosa Publishing House, India) vol.III, pp.1401 – 1406.
6. Richard P. Feynman, op.cit. p.667.
7. For instance, the root chakra at the base of the spine called Muldhara chakra is linked to matter or earth, the Swadhisthana chakra below the navel is linked to water, the Manipura chakra around the navel centre is linked to fire, the Anahata chakra in the heart region is linked to air, the Vishudha chakra at the throat level is linked to sound, and the Agya Chakra in the middle of eye brows is linked to light. The seventh Chakra at the top of head, called Sahasrara Chakra is the culmination and unification of all energy flow, and is considered to be like a thousand petal lotus flower opening up.

8. Motoyama, Hiroshi, *'Theories of the Chakras – Bridge to Higher Consciousness'* (1995, Theosophical Publishing House, USA).
   Also see:
   - Leadbeater, Charles W., *'The Chakras'* (2000, The Theosophical Publishing House, Chennai, India).
   - Talbot, Michael, *'Mysticism and the New Physics'* (1993, Penguin Books, London).
   - Collinge, Dr. William, *'Subtle Energy'* (1998, Harper Collins Publishers, London).
   - Sharamon, Shaila and Bodo J. Baginski, *'The Chakra Handbook'* (2000, Motilal Banarsidas Publishers, Delhi).
9. Ostrom, Joseph, *'Understanding Auras'* (1993, Harper Collins Publishers, London).
10. For an excellent description of electrical force working in human body, see: Guy Brown, *'The Energy of Life'* (1999, Harper Collins Publishers, London).
    For a discussion of cosmic radiation and energy, see: Paul Davies, *'Superforce'* (1995, Penguin Books, London) pp. 193 – 195.
11. For an excellent description of electro-magnetic force working in the cells, see: McFadden, Johnjoe, *'Quantum Evolution'* (2000, Harper Collins Publishers, London). This works because most of the cell membranes remain electrically polarized – with more positive ions outside the cell than inside it, resulting in a net negative voltage. In a normal state, the negative voltage difference in a cell is around (-)65 millivolt. When positive ions enter the membrane and cause electrical depolarization, the muscle and never cell respond.
12. For an interesting and elaborate discussion of this subject, see: Dr. William Collinge, op.cit. pp. 47 – 48.
13. *'Aitareya Upanishad'*, III – 1.3, translated by Swami Gambhirananda (1999, Advaita Ashrama, Calcutta), and *'Kena Upanishad'*, II.4, translated by Swami Gambhirananda (1998, Advaita Ashrama, Calcutta).
14. *'Mundaka Upanishad'* II.i.1 and 'Taittiriya Upanishad' III.i.1, both translated by Swami Gambhirananda (1995 & 1998, Advaita Ashrama, Calcutta).
15. Richard P. Feynman, *'Lectures on Physics'* (1998, Narosa Publishing House, India) vol.I, pp. 15, 47, 335.
16. Each spectrum of these frequencies is defined in terms of 'cycles', i.e. the number of oscillations of the wave per second. To give an example, the house-hold electric current has electro-magnetic waves of a very

low frequency of about 50 to 60 cycles per second. Radio waves which transmit radio signals have a frequency range of 500,000 to 1000,000 (half to one million) cycles per second. Light waves are in a much higher range. Those in the frequency range of 5×10^{14} to 5×10^{15} comprise the light spectrum which is visible to human eye. Those below this range are called infra-red and those above this range are called ultra-violet, both of which are not visible to the human eye but can be seen and measured by very sophisticated instruments. Electro-magnetic waves in still higher frequencies of 10^{18} and above are classified as X rays and Gamma rays. Those in the highest frequency range of 10^{27} and above are classified as Cosmic rays.

17. Quantum electro-dynamics (QED) explains the inter-action of photons and electrons. For a quantum mechanical description of inter-action between electro-magnetic field and matter by theory of Quantum electro-dynamics, see: Richard P. Feynman, 'QED: The Strange Theory of Light and Matter' (1985, Penguin Books, London).

18. According to field theory, the aggregate combined field of all sources is the sum of the fields of each source. This holds true because the field equations for electro-magnetic fields are differential equations which are linear. Since light field is known to be an electro-magnetic field, and Maxwell's differential equations for such fields are linear, these fields super-position. Their combined field is then described by the vector sum of all fields.

    For a very good description of field inter-actions according to quantum field theory, see: Gary Zukav, 'The Dancing Wu Li Masters' (1980, Bantam Books, New York) p. 199.

19. See: 'Mundaka Upanishad' II.ii.9 & 10, op.cit.

    Same idea is expressed in the following:

    – *'Katha Upanishad'* II.ii.15, translated by Swami Gambhirananda (2000, Advaita Ashrama, Calcutta) p. 115.

    – *'Viveka Chudamani'* op.cit. Sloka 128

    – *'The Bhagwad Geeta'*, translation and commentary by Swami -Chinmayananda (1969, Chinmaya Publications Trust, Madras) pp. 55, 83, 119.

20. Capra, Fritjof, *'The Web of Life'* (1996, Harper Collins Publishers, London) pp. 287 – 288.

21. Bohm, David, *'Wholeness and Implicate Order'* (1999, Routledge, London) pp. 19 – 20.

ABOUT THE AUTHOR

DR. RAMESH VAISH is an economist, chartered accountant, and lawyer. He has more than 45 years of experience in the fields of international finance, taxation and investments.

He did his M. A. in Accounting and Ph. D. in Economics at the University of Florida, USA. He has lived and worked in India, America, England and Singapore. Apart from his academic work, he has worked as Chairman of International Advisory Services – a division of Coopers & Lybrand in India – now merged with Price Waterhouse Coopers.

His previous book *'Our Existence – A Holistic View'* has been widely acclaimed in intellectual circles.